THIS IS NOT A RECIPE BOOK

TAL SPIEGEL

new Heroes & Pioneers

PHOTOGRAPHY:
NATHANAËL DJIMBILTH

Creativity follows curiosity

I almost died for this book.

I know that sounds extreme as the opening line for this book, but it's the truth.

While shooting the photos for this book, and after an exhausting week of work, I passed out for the first time in my life. Luckily, Nate, my photographer was there to catch me. Not only did I pass out, I was standing on a ladder when it happened! So yes, I see this book as a huge accomplishment, having risked my life for it.

Why am I telling you this? Firstly because – and I'm sure you'll all agree – it's a great dramatic opening, but also because I feel like this book put a lot of things into perspective for me. Things such as self-care, things about work, but mostly about passion. My passion for what I do, and how far I would go for my passion. Since I was a child, pastry has always been a big part of my life. I remember watching my mom working dough in the kitchen and admiring those movements of mixing, whipping, spreading, and folding. They were all magical to me.

As I grew up, I got to participate more and more in these majestic rituals of handmade desserts that made people so happy, and I loved it, it felt like my purpose from the get-go.

However, life took me on a different path. I was drawing and doing a lot of illustrating, too. When the time came to choose what I would study, I was contemplating between the world of pastry and the world of art & design and, at the time, my instinct was design. That choice took me on a four year journey of studying art and graphic design and, while some of you might wonder whether it was a waste of time given that, not long after I became a pastry chef, I can honestly tell you that I would probably never have become the pastry chef I am today without my background in graphic design.

My studies gave me perspective and taught me how to look at the world in a new way: through colour, form and composition. Suddenly everything you do has another aspect to it, and it's incredible. It's surreal, like having new superpowers that allow you to see the world in a completely different way.

Not long after I was working in the design industry, I knew pastry was my calling, and I moved to Paris.

Design gave me the tools to look at the creations I make, evaluate them and find the right balance in them.

Design gave me the tools to start my Instagram account *Desserted in Paris*, not because I wanted to be an 'instagrammer' or 'influencer', but because my designer side, recognised a need to apply these skills in a different way. I needed to create a pastry catalogue to use for my inspiration, and so, I started to document all the cakes I tried to make, mentioning the chef, the place and detailing the construction of the dessert... that was the beginning of my pastry encyclopedia – a tool that I, and thousands of people around the world, use in their search for inspiration and French pastry.

The more I evolved as a pastry chef, the more I understood the value of the combination of my two passions – design and pastry – and I believe that these two disciplines are what this book is all about.

I want to give you a glimpse into my head. I obviously can't directly teach you design or pastry, but I can show you my working methods, how I think like a designer when I create a dessert, and how I think like a pastry chef when I construct those ideas.

That's part of the reason for the name of this book. You can use it as a recipe book or a coffee table book, but my hope is to give you the tools to plan your next creation and help you obtain the best results.

It is very hard to show someone what is going on inside your head. What your thought processes are and where you draw inspiration from, what clicks that creative switch we all have inside of us.

My inspiration comes from all sorts of places: elements, flavours, places, tools, feelings and so on... but whatever they are, I take them, break them down and rebuild them into a creation that is unique to me, a creation that is "gourmand" and can start a conversation.

I can tell you now that, the source of my creations and work method is curiosity.

Curiosity often helps me find incredible solutions for creative briefs and it gets my brain working.

Curiosity makes you explore, read new material, try and test new things, and most importantly, learn from the process. Don't hesitate to search for something even if you think you know what it is in your head, you will be surprised to discover how many details you miss until you start to collect references and see visuals for your ideas...

Always remember, creativity follows curiosity.

Before we go on this journey and through the process of making these 15 creations, I firstly want to talk to you about the concept behind this book and how I think you should approach it.

As part of the initial conception for this book, I decided to use as many techniques and methods as possible:

I used existing moulds, I made new ones with a mould-making studio, I made moulds myself, I sculptured from modelling clay, I printed stencils, I tested 3D models and, of course, I sketched and wrote a lot to help my creative process.

I know you will not have some of the moulds in this book, and that's ok, as replicating these creations exactly isn't the point of this book.

You have the recipes, and you can take them and do what you want with them, in any shape or form you choose.

This is your very own creative challenge. So, please, take this book, take these recipes, and make them your own. I didn't have all the tools to create this book, but I experimented with everything at my disposal. I filled lemon squeezers with chocolate before I made a moulds from them, I built models and moulds from acetate paper and I spent hours in shops (and even hardware stores) and online to find new and interesting tools that I could

use (as you will see in the apple twist recipe).

Take this into consideration when you read this book, and keep an open mind so you can create your own work process, thought process and creative process. Exercising this, along with practising and developing your culinary imagination, will bring you better results, and the confidence to go all out on new, unique and spectacular creations.

Throughout the years, I have developed my skills and my methods of work, with the understanding that, it is one thing to know how to make desserts, but it's another thing to know how to be innovative, how to think outside the box and always reinvent yourself. We live in an age where it is very hard to invent something new in the pastry field, but it is much easier to improve the existing.

In my work for *Desserted in Paris*, I have shot hundreds of desserts throughout the years, and one day I decided to take all the lemon tarts I have photographed and put them together in one place. In doing this, I suddenly understood the power of creativity and self-expression. You take a simple creation, consisting of a base of dough, lemon cream and meringue, and you understand that the possibilities are endless. There's no one and only lemon meringue, and what you can do with it will be a new version of the existing, only different, creative, and essentially, yours.

I think that, apart from teaching masterclasses and exploring the pastry world, it's what I enjoy the most: collaborating with brands that ask me to create a dessert in the spirit of their

products. Whether it's a shoe, an alcohol brand or a chocolate brand, I get the chance to experience (almost) total creative freedom, that allows me to sail the waves of creativity and curiosity in my head.

And that is what this book is about. Challenging yourself to find inspiration in an object or anything else you can think of, and bring it to life.

You can choose what to take from this book: recipes, inspiration, or even just an enjoyable book by me with incredible photos by the talented Nate. As long as you can take *something* from it, my job of inspiring and 'turning-on' that creativity switch in you, is done.

Enjoy.
Tal

How to read the recipes

As I mentioned before, a lot of the creations in this book use special moulds that I have made myself hence, you will not find the sizes or instructions for a specific mould unless it is one that is readily available for purchase.

Feel free to use your imagination and creative side to build my desserts in your own personal way.

Gelatin mass: this is the mass of water mixed with gelatin powder, once set. I use fish-based gelatin. The ratio is 1:6 – for each 1 g of gelatin powder, I mix 6 g of water. Mix together until the gelatin is melted, and cool in the fridge until the gelatin mass hardens.

Guitar sheets: these are special transparent sheets used for chocolate work. Chocolate that crystallises on a sheet will have a strong shine.

Dough folds:
Simple fold: spread the dough into a rectangle, and visually divide the rectangle to 3 equal parts vertically. Fold toward the middle from the right side, and then fold the left top on top of it, creating a 3 layered dough.

Double fold: spread the dough into a rectangle and visually divide the rectangle to 4 equal parts. Fold toward the middle the right side and also fold towards the middle the left side. Then fold 2 sides together, creating a 4 layered dough.

Whipping attachment: the whisk that is used to whip. Inserting air into the body of the ingredient being worked with.

Paddle attachment: the attachment used to mix and beat.

Hook attachment: the one used for kneading doughs.

Make a crème pâtissière: to make a créme pâtissière, you need to mix the eggs and sugar (and whatever else is listed in the recipe). Bring the liquids to an almost boil, then temper the egg mix and hot liquids. This means, we don't want to pour all the eggs directly into the hot liquids because we have a good chance the eggs will solidify very quickly, and we'll be left with an omelette. By adding the hot liquids to the eggs first, and mixing, we raise the temperature of the eggs slowly. Therefore, we take around half of the hot liquid, pour it into the eggs and once all is well combined, we pour it back to the milk and mix everything together while stirring over medium heat until the cream thickens and starts to boil.

Make a crème anglaise: this involves pretty much the same process as described above, the only difference is that, after we temper the eggs and liquids and bring it all back to the heat, using a thermometer, we cook it to 82°C (without letting it boil) and then remove it from the heat. The result will be more liquid in consistency than the crème pâtissière, especially as it does not contain starch.

About the machines I have used:

All of these machines are pretty small and apt for at-home use as well.

Cutting printer: this is a machine used to cut stencils – and pretty much anything you want – using all types of materials. I use it mostly for cutting chocolate stencils.

Thermoforming machine: this is a machine I use to create moulds, especially for testing. While it makes great moulds, there's a limit to how much you can re-use the moulds as they are plastic and not silicone. If you need a reusable mould, you're better off making one out of silicone.

3D printer: I use this machine to create the shapes I need before putting them in the thermoform machine. With a resin-based 3D printer, I can make almost any shape I need and in any size while keeping the details accurate.

APPLE TWIST

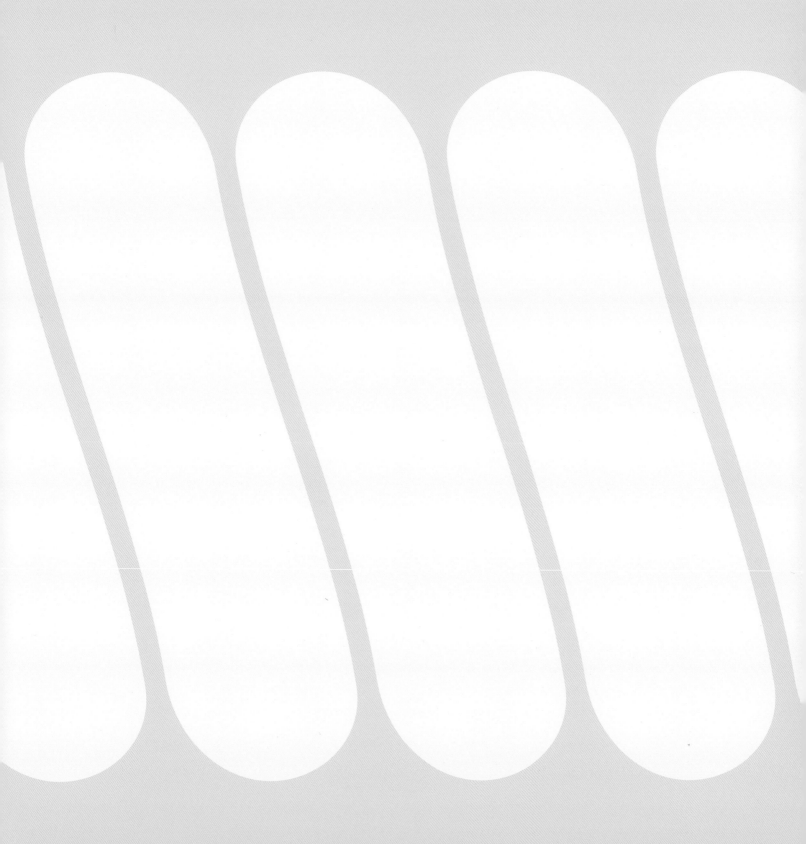

When I travel the world or even just my neighbourhood, I like to go to cooking shops, building supply stores, art supply shops or any shop with tools. I get inspired by tools and the possibility of creating something unique with a new find. You will be surprised by how many exceptional creations you can make using nonordinary tools.

So, when I came across this strange tool in some online video about potatoes, I fell in love with the shape it created and immediately I ordered it. It took a few trials, but when I got the hang of it, the apple twists came out looking so cool, I knew they could be the stars of my next apple creation.

Apple desserts are very high up on my list of all-time favourite desserts (along with lemon ones!). Something about their juiciness and contrasting acid-sweet flavour makes them the perfect fruit for desserts. I use them for viennoiserie, apple tarts, tarte tatin, strudel and so on, but this time I'm going to use them fresh to conserve that crunchy first bite.

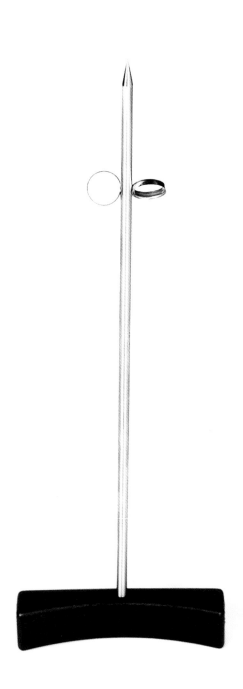

sumac

For my apple mood board, I'm looking at fresh flavours like mint, lemon, and obviously apples. I also want to add a tangy spice – sumac. Whilst they all have distinct flavours, none of them are particularly aggressive or too punchy. Hopefully they will harmonise and create the refreshing taste and bite effect I want to achieve for this dessert. Shapes of vintage jelly moulds and apple tart, apple cider and farm-homemade flavours are what inspired this dessert.

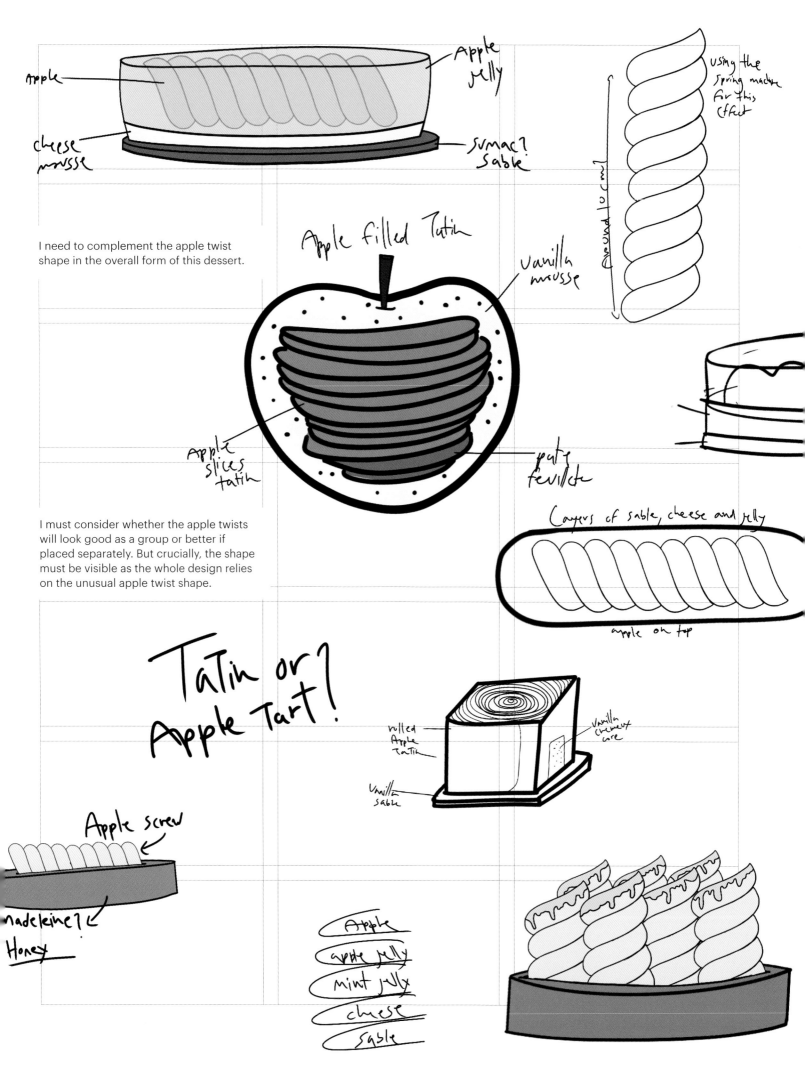

apple

cheese mousse

Apple Jelly

sumac? Sable

using the spring machine for this effect

around 10 cm

I need to complement the apple twist shape in the overall form of this dessert.

Apple filled Tatin

vanilla mousse

Apple slices tatin

pate feuillete

I must consider whether the apple twists will look good as a group or better if placed separately. But crucially, the shape must be visible as the whole design relies on the unusual apple twist shape.

Layers of sable, cheese and jelly

apple on top

Tatin or?
Apple Tart!

rolled Apple Tatin

vanilla cremeux core

Vanilla sable

Apple screw

madeleine?

Honey

Apple

apple jelly

mint jelly

cheese

sable

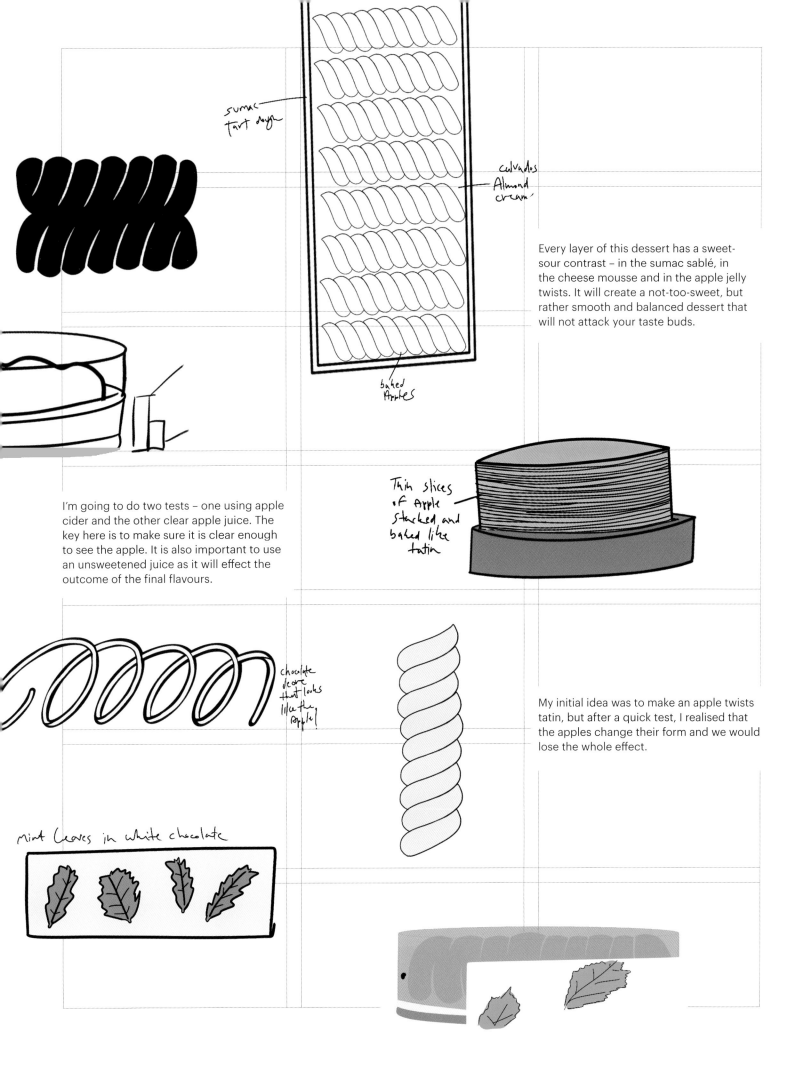

sumac tart dough

calvados Almond cream

baked Apples

Every layer of this dessert has a sweet-sour contrast – in the sumac sablé, in the cheese mousse and in the apple jelly twists. It will create a not-too-sweet, but rather smooth and balanced dessert that will not attack your taste buds.

Thin slices of Apple Stacked and baked like tatin

I'm going to do two tests – one using apple cider and the other clear apple juice. The key here is to make sure it is clear enough to see the apple. It is also important to use an unsweetened juice as it will effect the outcome of the final flavours.

chocolate decore that looks like the Apple!

My initial idea was to make an apple twists tatin, but after a quick test, I realised that the apples change their form and we would lose the whole effect.

mint leaves in white chocolate

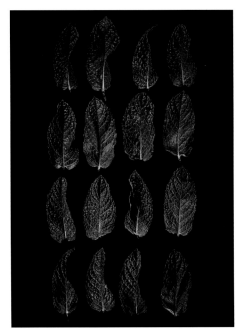
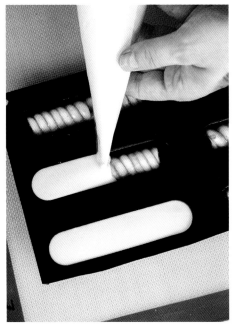
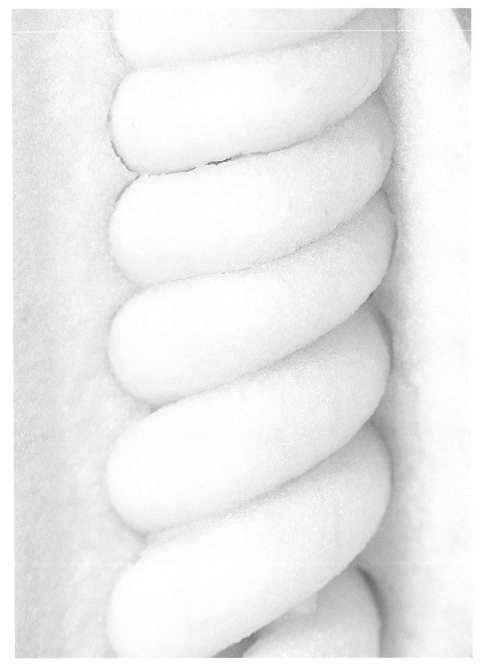

Apple infusion

800 g	water
175 g	sugar
10 g	lemon zest
5 g	ascorbic acid
2	Pink Lady apples

For the apples: each apple will make you around four screws, so about 2 apples is enough.

Mix all the ingredients together and then soak the apples in the infusion overnight.

Sablé sumac

370 g	flour
4 g	salt
120 g	almond powder
200 g	icing sugar
15 g	sumac
250 g	butter
90 g	eggs

In a stand mixer with paddle attachment, mix the flour, salt, almond powder, sugar, sumac and butter. Mix well until it reaches a sablé sand-like texture. Add the eggs slowly until well combined. Finally wrap in cling film and let rest over night before use.

Roll out the dough to 3 mm thickness and cut your desired shape with a cookie cutter. Bake between 2 "perforated" non-stick mats (silpain) at 160°C for around 20 minutes.

Apple jelly

200 g	clear, non sweetened apple juice
½	vanilla pod
2 g	agar agar
20 g	sugar
85 g	gelatin mass

Heat the apple juice and vanilla to 50°C, add the pre-mixed agar agar and sugar and mix slowly. Bring this to a boil, then add the gelatin mass and mix well.

Fromage blanc mousse

115 g	heavy cream (1)
55 g	sugar
27 g	yolks
150 g	white cheese (fromage blanc)
115 g	heavy cream (2)
27 g	gelatin mass

Heat the heavy cream (1) and make a crème anglaise (see page 7) with the sugar and yolks. Add the gelatin, mix well and let it cool. Mix this with the cheese and lemon. Finally, whip the heavy cream (2) and fold together.

Lemon mint jelly

200 g	water
30 g	fresh mint
20 g	lemon juice
38 g	gelatin mass
1 g	agar agar
15 g	sugar

Heat the water and mint and reduce until you have 80 g of mint water. Let this cool to 50°C, then add the sugar and agar agar. Bring this back to a boil and remove from the heat.

Add the gelatin and mix well.

Once combined, put the mixture through a sieve.

Decoration and construction

Zéphyr™ 34% white chocolate
fresh mint leaves

Also needed: a clear coating (nappage glaze) for finishing.

Make the lemon mint jelly and pour into the mould, to around 2 mm in height. Let this set in the fridge. Once set, place the apple on the lemon jelly and pour the apple jelly over it – to around 3/4 of the mould. Let this set in the fridge. Next, make the white cheese mousse and cover the jelly to the rim of the mould. Freeze.

Once frozen, remove from the mould. Cover with clear coating (nappage glaze) and place on the sumac sablé.

Make the chocolate decoration:
Pour the white chocolate on a guitar sheet. Place the mint leaves on top and cover with second guitar sheet.

Roll the chocolate with a rolling pin until it thins out. Cut in to your desired shape. Then place between two trays until it becomes firm.

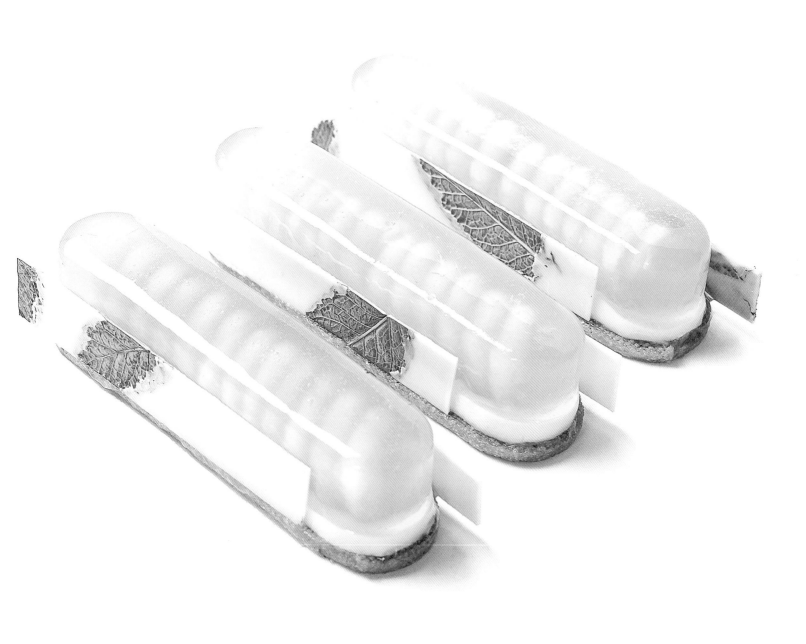

II

BAUHAUS

I was born in Tel Aviv, and I spent most of my life surrounded by Bauhaus buildings. Astonishingly enough, the city has almost 4000 Bauhaus structures, some protected under a preservation law. And to me, these buildings have always seemed like the white swans of Tel Aviv. Standing proud between some ugly 50s style constructions, the Bauhaus buildings are very easy to recognise with their smooth simple lines, and bright white appearance. While Tel Aviv is constructed of many types and forms of architecture including Arab influenced structures, art nouveau, art deco and American style skyscrapers, I have always found Bauhaus to be the most influential, that has earned Tel Aviv its second name "The White City".

Flashforward to my design studies, I related a lot of my work to Bauhaus, connecting my art design school work with the Bauhaus design school in Germany. The smooth flow of functional objects, the use of simple geometric shapes and the minimalism it reflects have always been intriguing to a colourful designer like me. I spent my years at design school trying to balance my relentless passion for rule-breaking, with the quietness and calmness of Bauhaus design, and this helped me gain that balance in my current work. When it came to pastry and especially this book, I knew I had to incorporate these elements and my knowledge thereof into a cake design.

What I want to bring to this creation is that meeting between German, minimalist design and the noise of a city that contains many cultures and influences. In Tel Aviv, you can find beautiful, renewed Bauhaus buildings but also old, neglected ones. You can find them on green pastoral boulevards but also along traffic-heavy main streets. It's this contrast I seek to find in my creation. What is there to say about Bauhaus? I want to take a piece of the city and jam it into that beautiful structure. Form vs functionality. I want to take that ugly 50s and 60s style and juxtapose it with some Bauhaus elements. Noise vs. silence. I'm going to find that balance of the white city and see it emerge in my design.

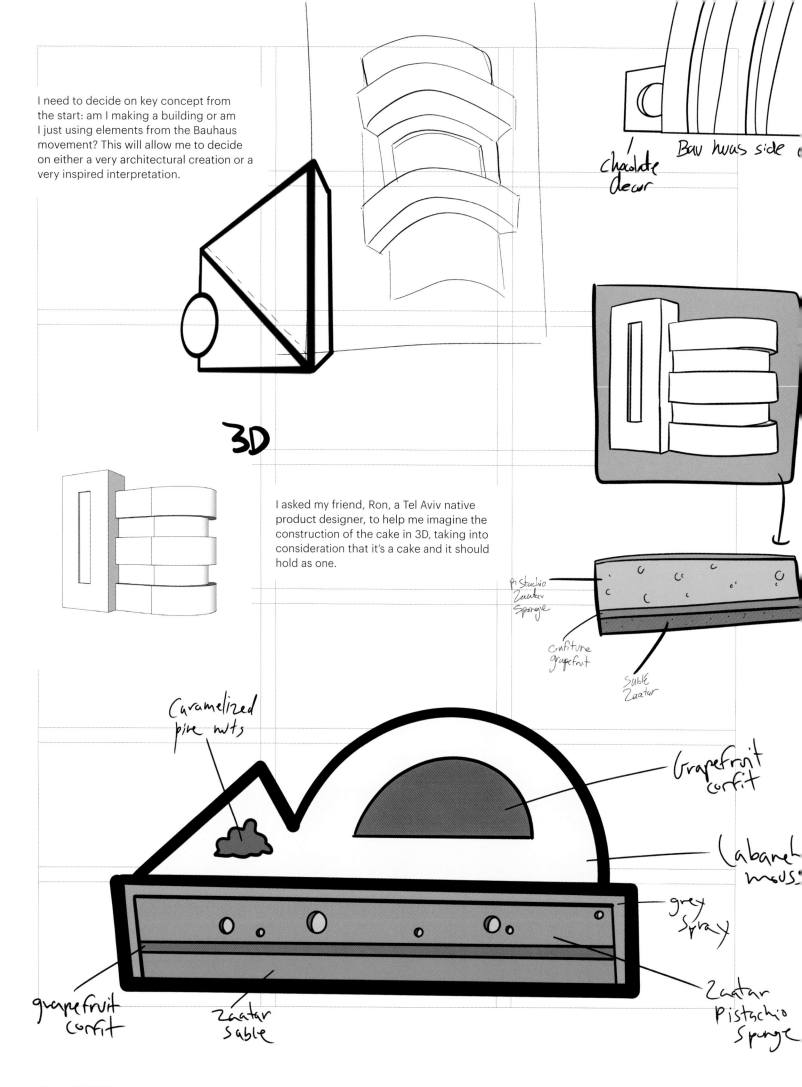

I need to decide on key concept from the start: am I making a building or am I just using elements from the Bauhaus movement? This will allow me to decide on either a very architectural creation or a very inspired interpretation.

Bau huas side

chocolate decor

3D

I asked my friend, Ron, a Tel Aviv native product designer, to help me imagine the construction of the cake in 3D, taking into consideration that it's a cake and it should hold as one.

Pistachio Zaatar Sponge

Confiture grapefruit

Sable Zaatar

Caramelized pine nuts

Grapefruit confit

Labaneh mousse

grey spray

Zaatar Pistachio Sponge

grapefruit confit

Zaatar Sable

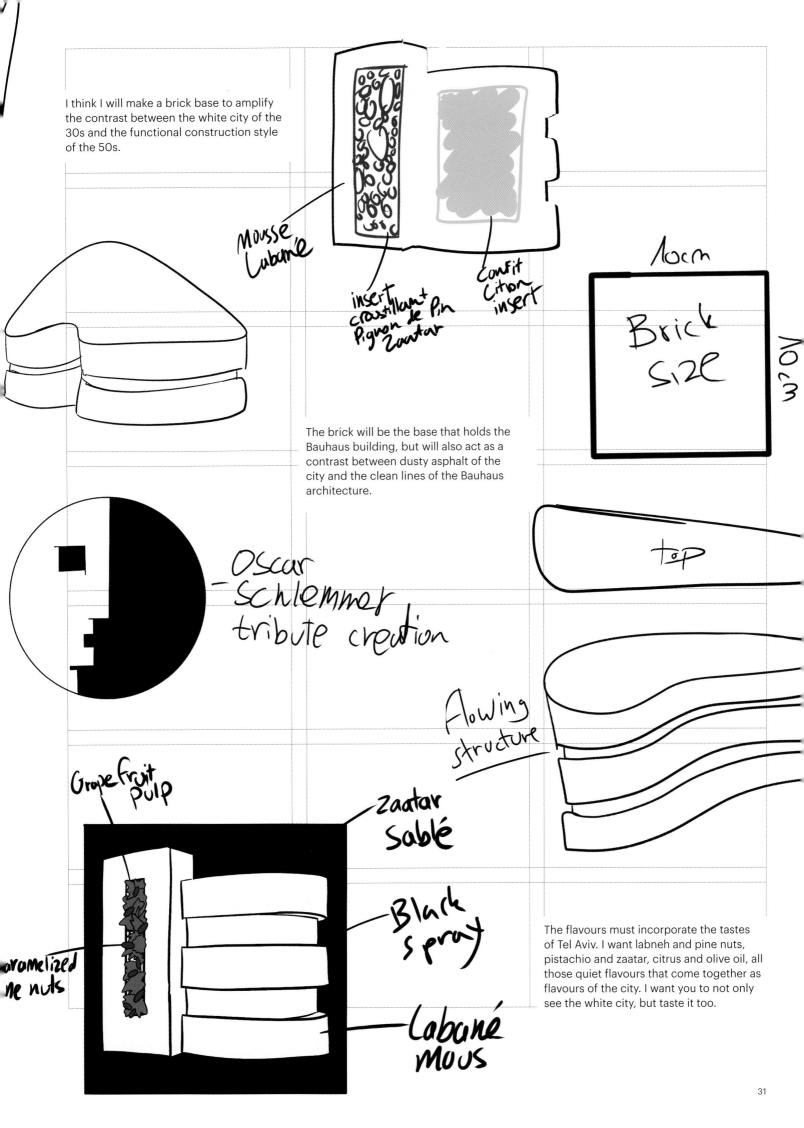

I think I will make a brick base to amplify the contrast between the white city of the 30s and the functional construction style of the 50s.

Mousse Labané

insert craustillant Pignon de Pin Zaatar

Confit Citron insert

10cm

Brick Size

10cm

top

The brick will be the base that holds the Bauhaus building, but will also act as a contrast between dusty asphalt of the city and the clean lines of the Bauhaus architecture.

Oscar Schlemmer tribute creation

Flowing structure

Grape fruit pulp

Zaatar Sablé

caramelized ne nuts

Black spray

The flavours must incorporate the tastes of Tel Aviv. I want labneh and pine nuts, pistachio and zaatar, citrus and olive oil, all those quiet flavours that come together as flavours of the city. I want you to not only see the white city, but taste it too.

Labané mous

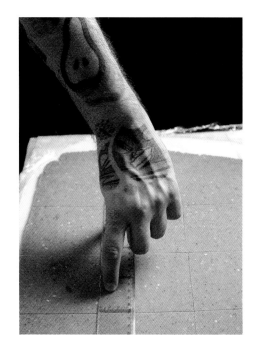

Zaatar sablé

380 g	flour
60 g	almond powder
15 g	zaatar
140 g	icing sugar
5 g	salt
210 g	cold butter
80 g	eggs

In a stand mixer, fitted with the paddle attachment, mix all ingredients, apart from the eggs, to form a sand-like texture. Add the eggs slowly until well combined.

Cover in cling film and chill overnight in the fridge. Roll the dough out 2 mm thick and cut it in squares. Bake at 160°C for around 20 minutes between 2 silpains or until golden.

Caramelised pine nuts

150 g	pine nuts
100 g	sugar
25 g	water

Bring the sugar and the water to 118°C. Add the pine nuts and mix until caramelised.

Pour over a silicone mat while carefully separating the nuts as much as possible. Let it cool.

Grapefruit confit

90 g	grapefruit juice
3 g	pectin NH
3 g	grapefruit zest
45 g	sugar
180 g	fresh grapefruit supremes

Heat the grapefruit juice and the zest to 50°C and add to the preparation the sugar and the pectin previously combined together. Mix well, bring to a boil and let it cool for a few minutes. Incorporate the fresh grapefruit supremes and let cool.

Zaatar sponge

130 g	flour
40 g	almond powder
300 g	eggs
120 g	sugar
40 g	inverted sugar
40 g	tahini
12 g	zaatar
15 g	olive oil

Sift together the flour, the almond powder and the zaatar and set aside. In a stand mixer with the paddle attachment, beat the eggs, the sugar and the inverted sugar until a light mixture forms. Add the dry ingredients in the mixer bowl and continue mixing just until well combined.

Gradually add the olive oil and the tahini and mix until well combined. Pour into a frame to 1 cm thickness and bake at 190°C for 6–7 minutes. Cut into squares, the same size as the sablé squares.

Labaneh mousse

100 g	labaneh (1)
60 g	sugar
36 g	gelatin mass
150 g	labaneh (2)
15 g	olive oil
10 g	lemon juicepuree
230 g	heavy cream

Bring the labaneh (1) and the sugar to a boil. Add the gelatin and mix. Add the labaneh (2) and mix again. Add the oil and the lemon juice, and mix well with a hand blender.

Whip the heavy cream and fold it into the preparation.

White spray

80 g	Zéphyr™ 34% white chocolate
100 g	cacao butter
	white colouring

Melt the cacao butter and the white chocolate to 34°C. Add the colouring and mix with a hand blender before spraying with spray gun.

Decoration and construction

Ocoa™ 70% dark chocolate
Zéphyr™ 34% white chocolate
white colouring
black colouring

Pipe the labaneh mousse in mould until halfway. Pipe the grapefruit confit on one side of the mould, and spread some caramelised pine nuts on the other side. Cover with more labaneh mousse. Freeze. Once frozen, spray with the white spray.

In a square frame, a little bigger than the bauhaus mould size, place the zaatar sponge. Cover with a layer of the grapefruit confit and top with the zaatar sablé. Freeze completely.

Once frozen, remove from the frame and using a microplane, grate the 4 sides of the frozen block, to straighten it and slightly reduce its size.

In the same size square frame, line the bottom with cling film. Pour a small amount of tempered melted white chocolate and spread it evenly to cover the film and the sides of the frame.

Once the white chocolate is spread, place the frozen block with the sablé facing up.

Push the block down gently, so that the chocolate stars to come out from the top edges, and until the top of the block aligns with the top of the frame.

Clean the excess chocolate and let set. Remove gently from the frame and spray with the grey spray.

To make the grey spray: use the same recipe as for the white spray and add a little bit of black colouring.

Using a knife and a brush, spread some white and black colour splashes to obtain an asphalt texture.

Place the Bauhaus part on top.

III

FLAMINGO

My love for 'flamingo pastry' started a few years ago when I wanted to create a new version of the classic swan chou. But, as always, I wanted to give this my own twist by recreating a very well-known pastry with a different bird.

I love flamingos, their vibrant colour (yep, I'm a sucker for pink) which they actually get from eating shrimps and seaweed, and their character (look up their mating dance) make them quite a fun and interesting bird to me.

While working on the flamingo sketches I passed by an ad on the street that featured a flamingo pool float in it. I took a photo of it and thought it could be an interesting new version of the existing idea I was working on. Plus, who doesn't love those huge inflatable flamingo floats? That made me resketch the flamingo, and try to find new solutions while keeping the flamingo as my inspiration, just changed the direction of where I wanted this dessert to go (or float).

For this specific dessert, I spent a lot of time observing flamingo videos. I wanted to capture their essence and character. I wanted my flamingo float to look like the closest thing to a flamingo as possible by capturing the right colour mix of pink, black and white, the ratio between the float and the head, and of course making it look as real as possible.

Flamingos are such mysterious animals, they're not your common bird that you see often, but still, humans are fascinated by them, and for the past few years they've been showing up everywhere! Lamps, decorations, clothes and of course floats.

I remember that scene in *Alice in Wonderland* where Alice is playing a croquet game, and it always makes me laugh, how you can take such a creature and give it such a comedic character. I think that's what the flamingo float is all about.

The hardest part will be to capture that neck shape and connect it with the base. It's challenging but it's the kind of challenge I love: creating something out of nothing but imagination and cooking techniques.

For the flavours, I'm going with cherry and baharat, which is a Middle Eastern mix of spices, typically used for meat and different kinds of food. This combination will give this dessert a unique twist.

wing?

tonka chantilly

chocolat feathers

tonka cherry confit

cherry cremeux

Pâte a choux

meringue Swiss

choco ro

chocolat noir

chou

Parfum:
Tonka Cerise
confit cerise tonka
cremeux cerise

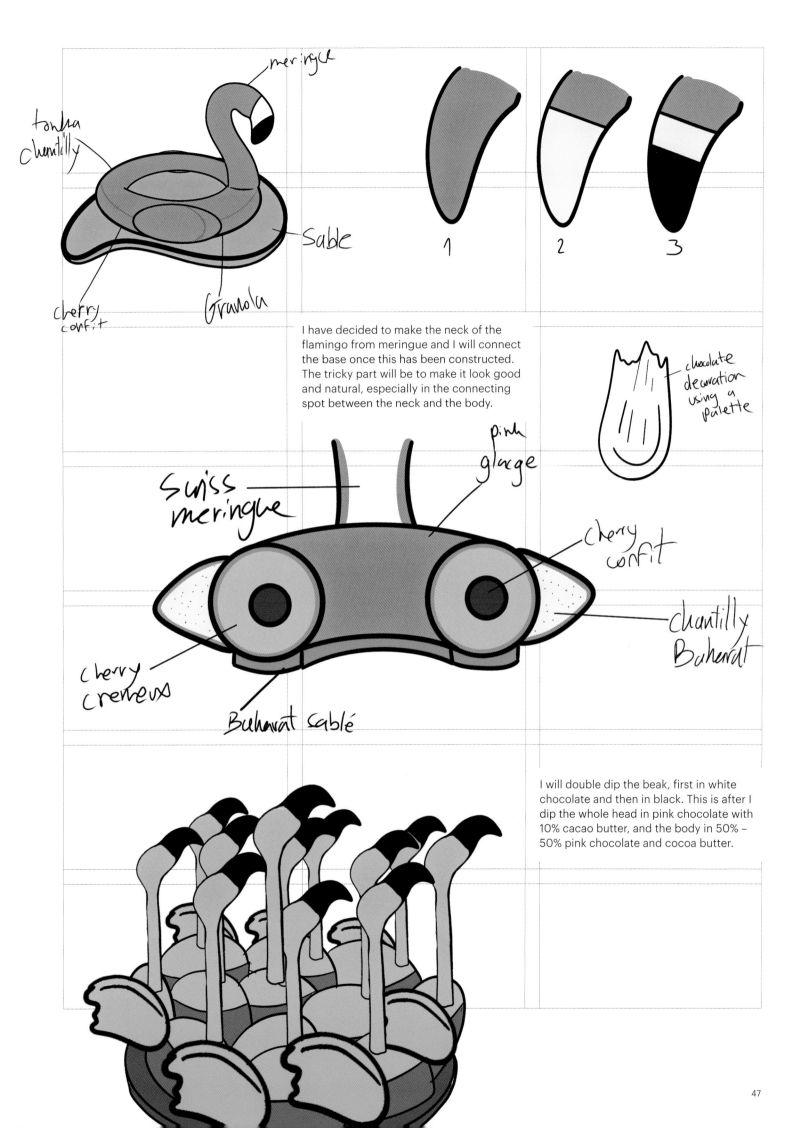

meringue

tonka
chantilly

Sable

cherry
confit

Granola

1   2   3

I have decided to make the neck of the
flamingo from meringue and I will connect
the base once this has been constructed.
The tricky part will be to make it look good
and natural, especially in the connecting
spot between the neck and the body.

chocolate
decoration
using a
palette

pink
glacge

Swiss
meringue

cherry
confit

chantilly
Baharat

cherry
cremeux

Baharat Sablé

I will double dip the beak, first in white
chocolate and then in black. This is after I
dip the whole head in pink chocolate with
10% cacao butter, and the body in 50% –
50% pink chocolate and cocoa butter.

Baharat sablé

180 g	flour
75 g	almond powder
3 g	bicarbonate
110 g	butter
80 g	sugar
4 g	baharat
60 g	eggs

In a stand mixer with the paddle attachment, mix all the ingredients together apart from the eggs. Once combined and a sand-like texture has formed, add the eggs slowly until well incorporated.

Wrap in plastic and let this cool in fridge overnight. Cut into doughnut shaped pieces, and bake at 170°C between two silpains for around 12 minutes or until golden.

Baharat chantilly

120 g	heavy cream (1)
20 g	trimoline
12 g	gelatin mass
25 g	mascarpone
3 g	baharat
140 g	heavy cream (2)

In a saucepan, bring the cream (1), baharat and trimoline to a boil. Remove from the heat, add the gelatin mass, mix and pour over the mascarpone. Add the cream (2), mix well with a hand blender and then leave overnight to cool in fridge before whipping.

Cherry crémeux

120 g	milk
65 g	heavy cream
150 g	cherry puree
75 g	yolks
35 g	sugar
34 g	gelatin mass

In a saucepan, heat cream, milk, and cherry puree to an almost boil. Mix the yolks and sugar in a separate bowl and make a crème anglaise (see page 7). Remove from heat, add gelatin, strain and cool in the fridge overnight.

Cherry confit

150 g	cherry puree
25 g	inverted sugar
15 g	sugar
2.5 g	pectin NH
7 g	lemon juice

Bring the cherry puree and inverted sugar syrup to 50°C, and add the pre-mixed sugar and pectin while stirring. Bring to a boil for 1 minute, then remove from heat. Add the lemon juice and mix. Cover with cling film and let it cool completely.

Swiss meringue

100 g	egg whites
200 g	icing sugar

In a bain-marie, heat the egg whites and icing sugar to 50°C while gently stirring with a whisk (but not whisking!). Transfer to a stand mixer with the whipping attachment and whip until firm. Pipe flamingo shapes, as seen in the making off pages of the recipe, with a size 10 piping tip. Bake at 80°C for around 2 hours or until firm and dry. Let them cool completely.

Pink dipping glaçage for crémeux

250 g	Zéphyr™ 34% white chocolate
250 g	cacao butter
	red colouring

Melt the chocolate and cacao butter then add the colouring and mix with a hand blender. Cool the mixture to 34°C before dipping the cake.

Decoration and construction

Zéphyr™ 34% white chocolate
Ocoa™ 70% dark chocolate
red food colouring
black food colouring
white food colouring

Pipe crémeux into a doughnut shaped mould, add in the cherry confit insert or pipe gently. Finish with piping more crémeux on top of the confit and freeze. Keep any leftover crémeux aside. Next, for the wings, whip the baharat chantilly and pipe it into a quenelle mould before freezing.

Once frozen, connect the doughnut and the wings together using some crémeux and then freeze again. Once frozen, dip into the pink dipping glaçage. Finally, place over baked sablé rings.

Dip the meringue flamingos in pink chocolate. If the chocolate is too thick, add some melted cocoa butter. Let this harden before dipping the beak in white chocolate. Let this harden. Next, dip the extremity of the beak black chocolate.

Finally, using some chocolate, and chocolate cooling spray, connect the head to the body.

IV

FLOWER

This dessert is very different from the others in this book, and from those I usually make in general – which is part of the reason why I chose it. I'm not going to reinvent the wheel with the babka, everyone makes babkas – my mom makes them, my Grandma made them... I basically grew up with babkas all around me. But what I do want to take a crack at with the babka, is its quintessential qualities.

Most people go through the same motions to get the babka look, by rolling the dough with the chocolate, cutting the roll in half and twisting the two halves together. I want to break this formulaic system and create a beautiful babka that offers a new take on the taste experience. I remember as a kid, standing next to my mom, watching her spread the chocolate over the elastic dough, rolling it slowly, cutting and twisting it, and finally brushing it with some syrup after it baked.

Apart from the chocolatey smells that took over the neighbourhood, I was fascinated by the process. I would ask my mom, every single time, to let me spread the chocolate and roll the dough. This precious memory has stayed with me to this day and it is why I respect the process of the babka, but still, I want to break the babka apart and rebuild it into something new, that is my take on it. To create my own babka process, if you will.

I want to test how does a new shape might potentially affect the taste of the babka. I want to try a new technique and explore new flavour combinations. The way I see it, sometimes changing the technique could effect the flavours drastically.

I've been watching a lot of videos on how to make Chinese dumplings and I'm always fascinated by the hand gestures used to create them. It is an art in itself – working with dough and bending it to your will. I'm certainly drawing my inspiration from working with the dough in this manner. However, I still want to honour the memory of the delicate way my mom worked the dough and include even more softness and movement to the way it's constructed. I want to create a kind of babka flower, by taking the two elements– dough and chocolate – and making something new with these classic ingredients.

Babka
Dumpling
filled with
chocolate?

So much of the babka made today is created with store-bought chocolate spread. I can totally see why – it's ready-made and works great with baked dough – but I want to make my own chocolate spread to introduce that level of distinction to the flavours of my babka.

Bowl

Roll into a flower roll
and place in ring

classic roll

babka Dough

green buckwheat

chocolate nibs

chocolate spread

I know I want to add an element of crunch to the babka, but instead of the classic hazelnut, I will use baked green buckwheat. This will add a soft crunch to the bite and add another layer of flavour to the babka.

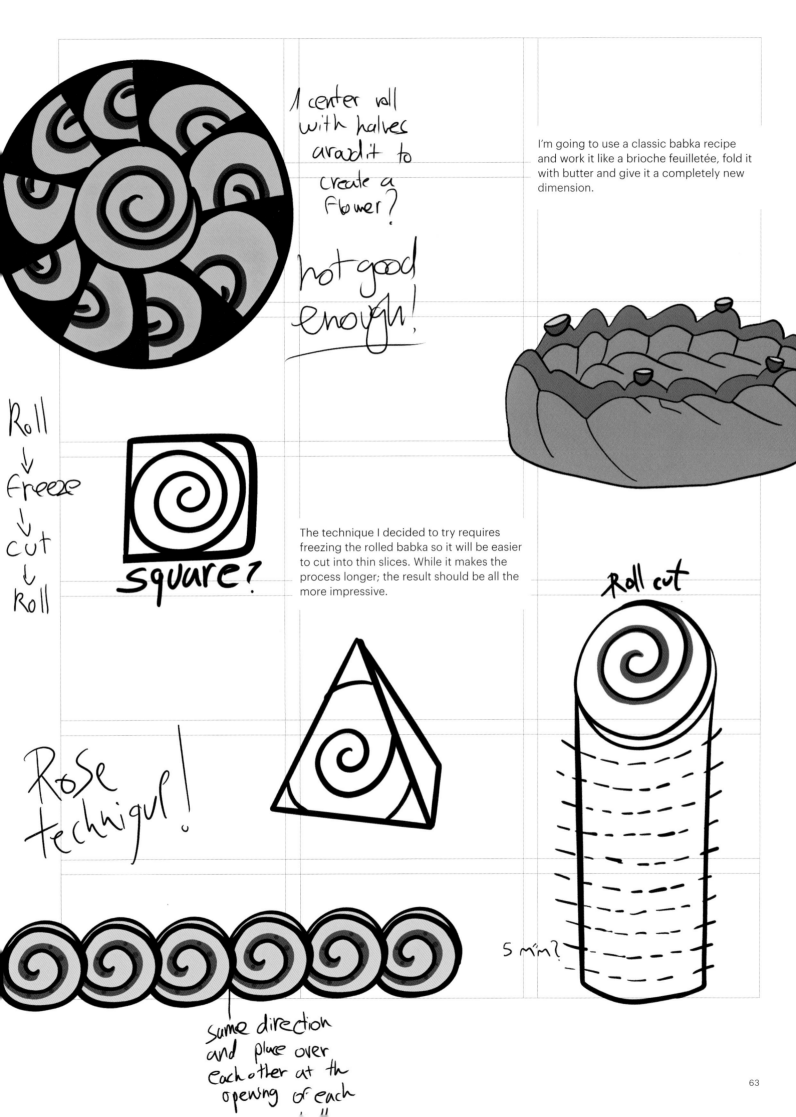

1 center roll with halves around it to create a flower?

not good enough!

I'm going to use a classic babka recipe and work it like a brioche feuilletée, fold it with butter and give it a completely new dimension.

Roll
↓
Freeze
↓
Cut
↓
Roll

square?

The technique I decided to try requires freezing the rolled babka so it will be easier to cut into thin slices. While it makes the process longer; the result should be all the more impressive.

Roll cut

Rose technique!

5 min?

same direction and place over each other at the opening of each

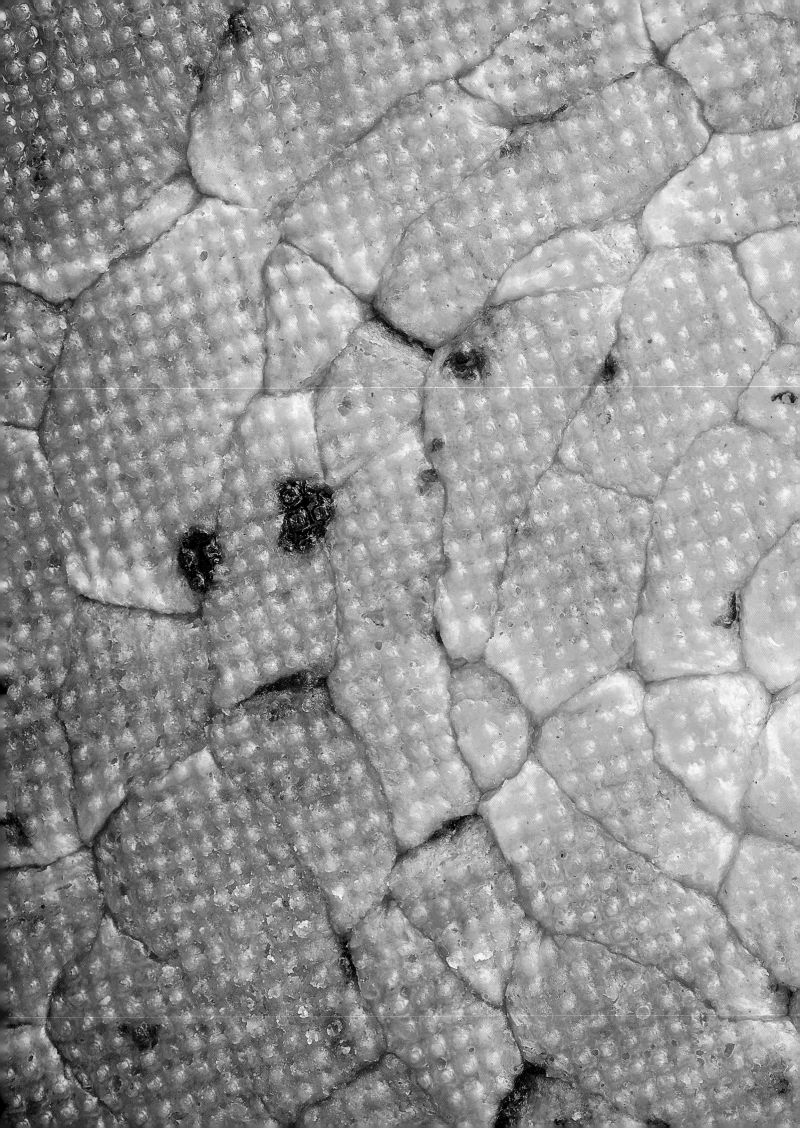

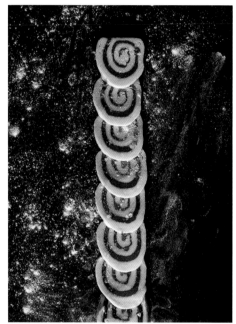

Dough

115 g	milk
18 g	fresh yeast
65 g	sugar
82 g	eggs
470 g	flour
2 g	salt
70 g	soft butter
180 g	butter for folding
	egg for brushing

In a bowl of a stand mixer, mix slightly warm milk with fresh yeast, add sugar, eggs, flour and salt and mix all using the hook attachment.

When combined, slowly add the soft butter and continue to mix well on medium speed until dough is smooth and elastic. Let dough rest outside for a couple of minutes, in a bowl covered with plastic wrap. Then transfer to fridge for 4 hours or overnight.

Roll the dough in a square shape of about 30 x 30 cm. Prepare the butter in a square by putting it between 2 sheets of parchemin paper, and roll it in a square shape of about 17 x 17 cm.

Place the butter on top of the dough at a 45 degree angle. Then close the dough over the butter by taking the corners of the dough and bring them towards the center. Finally roll the dough in a rectangle shape and fold as such:

Simple fold, simple fold and finally double fold, letting it rest 1 hour minimum between each fold.

To understand the process of folding, please refer to page 3.

Buckwheat praliné

225 g	toasted almonds
225 g	toasted hazelnuts
200 g	toasted green buckwheat
325 g	sugar
80 g	water
8 g	vanilla
4 g	salt

Cook the sugar and water to 118°C.

Add the almonds and hazelnuts and mix well until caramelised. Pour over silicone mat and let it cool. Add the buckwheat, salt and vanilla to a food processor and blitz until it forms a paste.

Chocolate buckweat spread

450 g	milk chocolate gianduja
540 g	buckwheat praliné
25 g	milk powder
35 g	cacao powder
80 g	pure hazelnut paste
100 g	Ocoa™ 70% dark chocolate
10 g	vanilla extract

In a bain-marie, melt the gianduja and the dark chocolate. Put with all ingredients in a food processor and blitz until it forms a paste. Let it rest a couple of hours before using, so the paste thickens.

Syrup

120 g	water
110 g	sugar

Bring all to boil and then let the mixture cool slightly.

Decoration and construction

toasted buckwheat & chocolate chips for spreading

Roll the dough out to about 50 x 30 cm and spread with the Pâte à tartiner, toasted buckwheat and chocolate chips. Cut into 4 equal rectangles and roll each one of them out. Cover in cling film and freeze for 2 hours.

Take the dough out of the freezer and cut into 4 mm thick slices, making a strip of 6–8 slices covering each other's opening (like in the photo in the making off page). Press lightly with a rolling pin to stick them together, and roll; repeat the process rolling the new strip over the last one you have placed, in order to make the flower bigger. You need to make sure you always work in the same direction of the slices until the flower is created. Brush with egg, proof for 2 hours, brush with egg again and then bake at 190°C for 25 minutes.

Brush with syrup immediately.

Optional: decorate with tempered chocolate disk and toasted buckwheat.

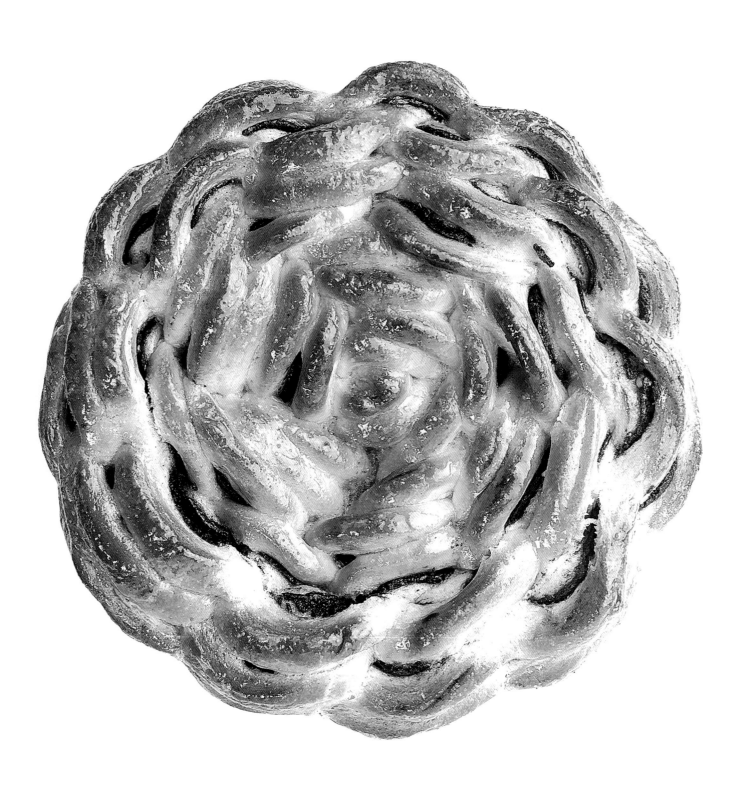

V

CORAL REEF

I have a mould that is meant for decorating big cakes. One day, I saw it in a completely different light. It's strange how inspiration can suddenly strike and on this day, it certainly did. I looked at the mould and immediately thought to myself "this mould must be used for an ocean inspired dessert". It very much reminded me of a coral reef as it has an aquatic look to it that captivated me.

I don't spend much time on the coast and I have never been scuba diving as I'm much more of a mountain kind of guy. But there's a irrefutable quiet beauty to the ocean that I really wanted to tap into with this dessert. The magnificence of underwater coral fields and the endless colour schemes became a huge inspiration. Furthermore, there are so many different coral shapes and colours to play with.

Looking at this mould, the first dessert that came to mind was a Pavlova (based on the Russian ballerina, Anna Pavlova). For me, this dessert and the coral reefs share similar characteristics – delicate movements, beautiful shapes, and wonderful expression. Then there is the texture: crunchy meringue, a creamy filling and an acid sweetness that wraps around your tongue with each bite that you take.

As I already mentioned in the introduction, the options for colours and shapes are endless. At the moment, I am trying to focus and find inspiration in the feeling a coral reef leaves me with. Nature has created these bouquets of underwater flowers and I find them so mesmerising. In terms of colour, I think it is going to have to be a red – a perfect choice as it ties in well with the red fruits I want to use.

chocolate coral decor
with blueberries on it?

How do i make it look

on top
of a cake!

more like a coral reef

For the flavours, I want to play with red
fruits. A raspberry meringue, red fruit
cream and blueberry gel.

For the confit:
—Piping
—squeezer
—paper cornet

gold
leaf

I'm going to try a few decoration styles:
chocolate corals, coloured tuilles, real
flowers and even a coral dome. I don't want
to overload this dessert as it needs to be
elegant but I will try different directions to
see what will work best.

For the meringue, to match the shape of
the mould, I will create a gelatin mould
and sketch from it the outer shape of the
pavlova. It's a bit of work, but it will ensure
a good result and will help me place the
top part of the pavlova on the meringue
easily.

chocolate Sea plants
pipe chocolate in ice water?

or create a
moving calp cake

needs special
mould

hot
will

A chocolate dome
filled with red fruit confit
and piped with vanilla chantilly

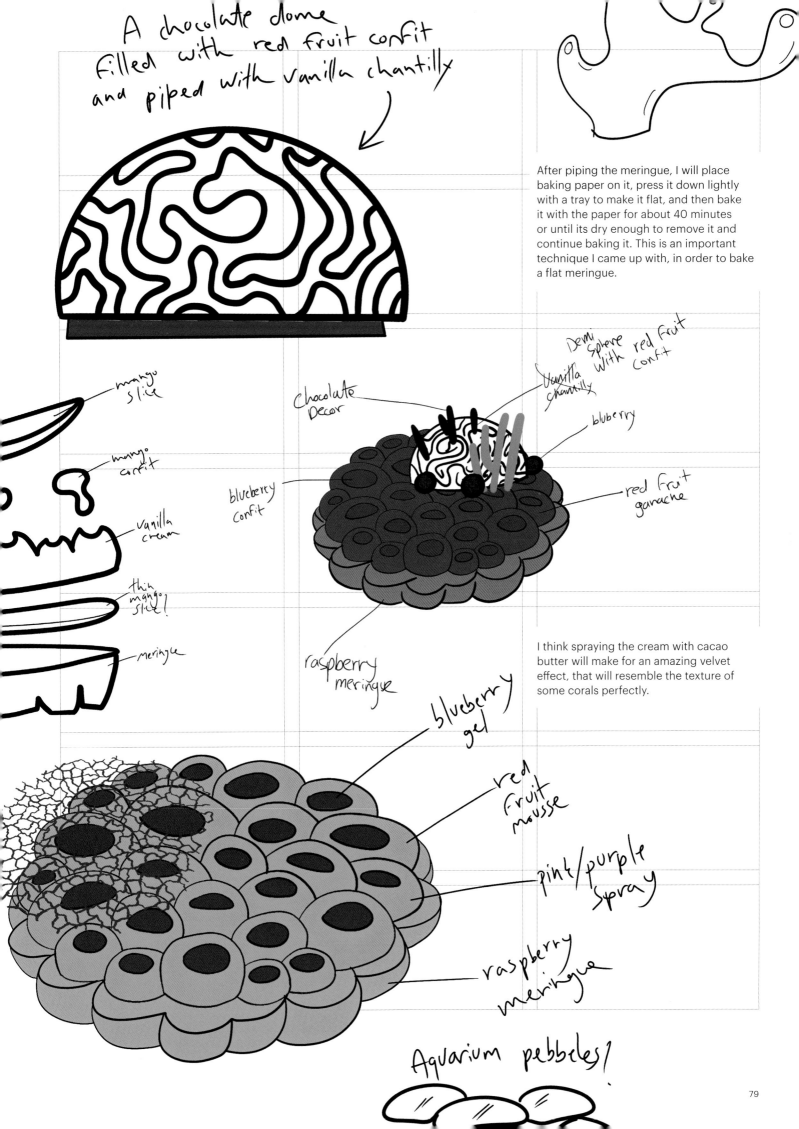

After piping the meringue, I will place baking paper on it, press it down lightly with a tray to make it flat, and then bake it with the paper for about 40 minutes or until its dry enough to remove it and continue baking it. This is an important technique I came up with, in order to bake a flat meringue.

mango slice

mango confit

vanilla cream

thin mango slice!

meringue

Chocolate Decor

blueberry Confit

raspberry meringue

Demi Sphere with red fruit confit

Vanilla chantilly

bluberry

red fruit ganache

I think spraying the cream with cacao butter will make for an amazing velvet effect, that will resemble the texture of some corals perfectly.

blueberry gel

red fruit mousse

pink/purple spray

raspberry meringue

Aquarium pebbles!

79

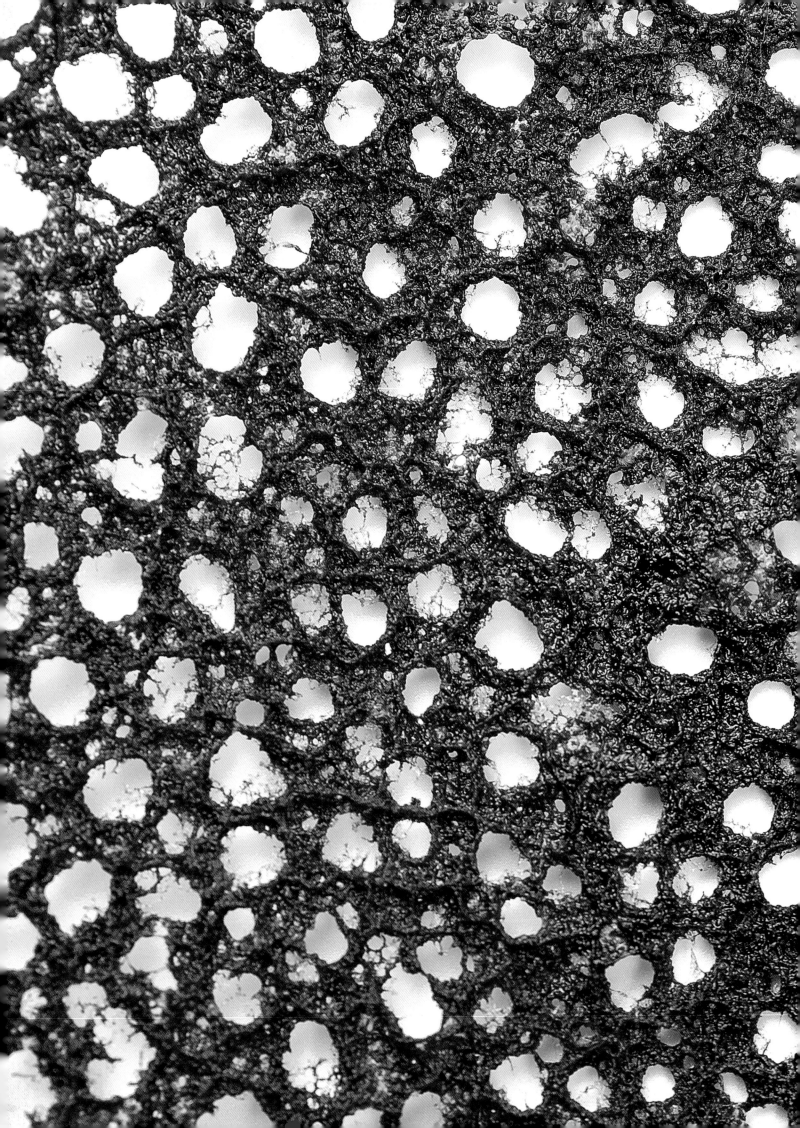

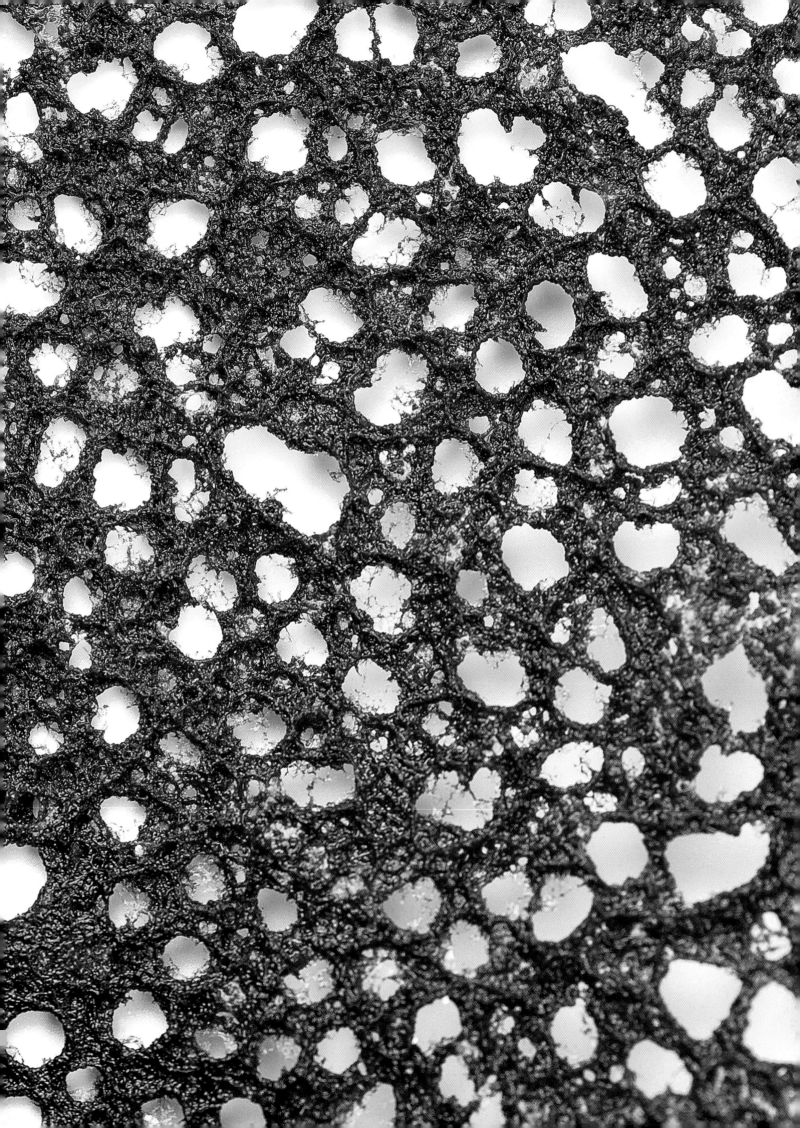

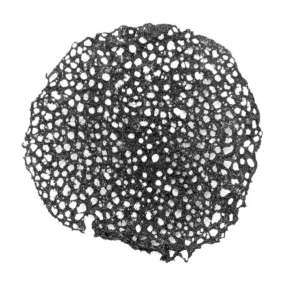

Raspberry Swiss meringue

420 g   icing sugar
210 g   egg whites
20 g   raspberry powder

In a bain-marie, heat the egg whites, icing sugar and raspberry powder to 55°C while constantly stirring with a whisk (but not whisking!). Once at temperature, move to a stand mixer with the whipping attachment and whip the egg whites until firm.

Move the mixture into a piping bag with a size 10 round piping tip and pipe immediately on a baking sheet in the shape of the pavlova you have created with the cardboard (see sketches pages of the recipe). Place parchment paper over the top of the meringue and, straighten the meringue by gently pressing down on it with a tray. Bake at 80°C with the paper on top for the first hour and then gently remove the paper, before continuing to bake at 80°C for 2–3 hours or until dry.

Blueberry gel

300 g   blueberry puree
60 g   inverted sugar
35 g   lemon juice
32 g   gelatin mass

In a saucepan, bring the blueberry puree and inverted sugar to an almost boil. Remove from the heat, add the lemon juice and the gelatin mass. Mix.

Let it cool completely, then mix well with a hand blender.

Tuille

10 g   flour
55 g   water
20 g   icing sugar
60 g   grapeseed oil
         water based purple colouring

Combine and mix all the ingredients with a hand blender.

Next, heat a saucepan and fry a spoonful of the tuille mix until dry. Place it on a paper towel to remove the excess oil. Repeat until all used.

Red fruit mousse

75 g   milk
45 g   yolks
35 g   gelatin mass
55 g   sugar
160 g   red fruit puree
115 g   heavy cream

In a stand mixer with the whipping attachment, whip the heavy cream in bowl. Set aside.

In a saucepan, heat the milk. Separately in a bowl, mix the yolks and sugar and make a crème anglaise (see page 7).

Add the gelatin and pour over the red fruit puree.

Next, mix with a hand mixer and let it cool completely.

Fold gently together with the whipped cream. Pipe into the mould and freeze.

Purple spray

80 g   Zéphyr™ 34% white chocolate
100 g   cacao butter
         purple colouring

Melt the cacao butter and the white chocolate to 34°C. Add the colouring and mix with a hand blender before spraying with spray gun.

Decoration and construction

Remove the mouse from the mould and spray with the purple spray.

Place over the meringue and fill the holes with the blueberry gel. Place the tuille on the top.

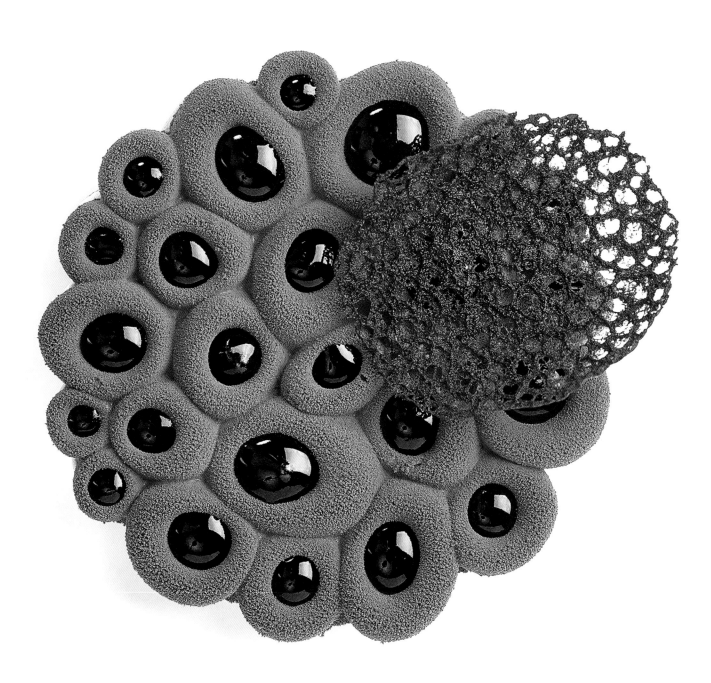

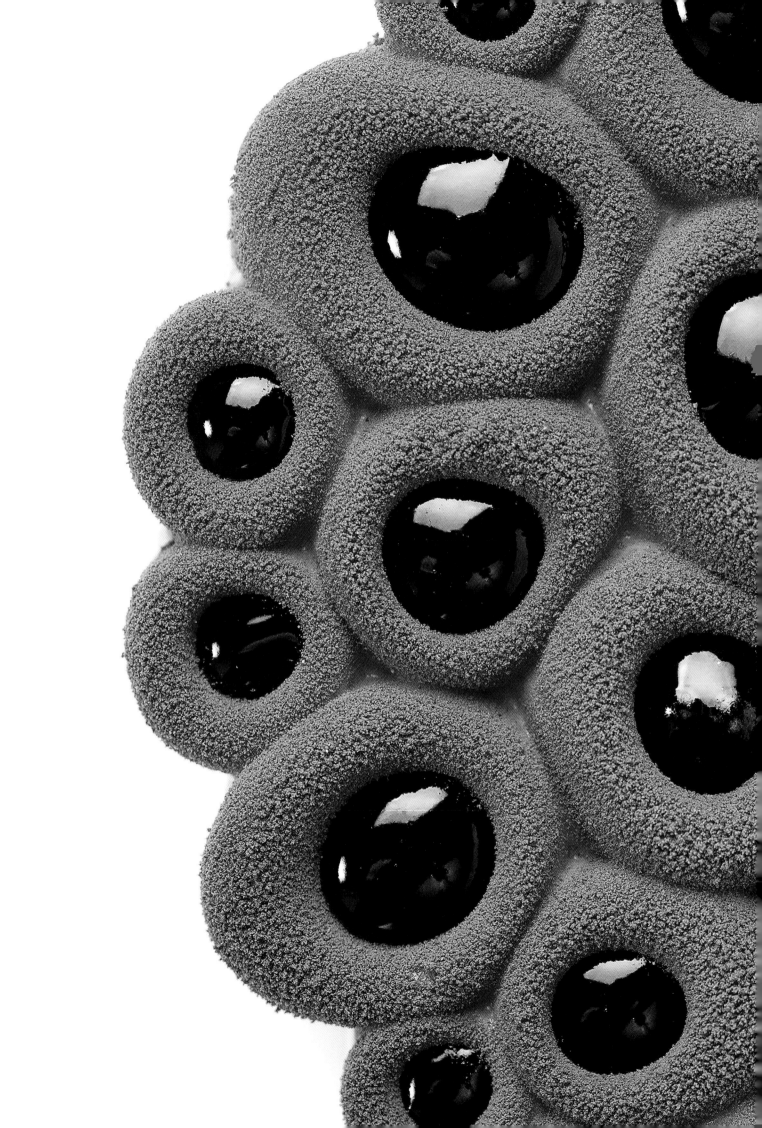

VI

LEMON SQUEEZER

I have always been fascinated with lemon tarts, primarily because lemon meringue tart is probably my favourite dessert in the world, but more than that, I find it to be one of the most balanced desserts of all time. Texture wise – crunchy dough, creamy curd and airy meringue – a gradient of textures from hard to soft, providing the perfect bite. And flavour wise – almondy and earthy dough, acid fruity curd and sweet meringue. The whole combination creates the perfect balance.

One day, whilst working on the presentation for my "creative routine" lecture, I wanted to show people how my Instagram account "desserted_in_paris" have created the catalogue of Parisian desserts, all of which embody the mood and style of what I wanted to design. So, with this in mind, I took all the lemon tarts I had shot in the past five years and put them together on one page. The results astonished me. When you put all those lemon tarts together – the unlimited amount of creativity and possibilities gained from those three key elements become evident! And that got me thinking: what was my signature lemon tart? I wanted to create a lemon tart that would not only represent my love for this dessert, but one that would also reflect my creative side when relying on these basic elements to create this exquisite dessert.

Through my observation and fascination with lemon tarts (which is really quite extensive), I've noticed how it has become "trendy" to make lemon tarts in the shape of a lemon slice, or a lemon half. But I didn't want to just jump on the bandwagon and do the same, I wanted to find inspiration elsewhere. Over the countless hours of making and baking my own lemon tarts, one of the common denominators were my lemon squeezers. And it dawned on me: Whilst they all serve the same purpose, they are all intrinsically different in design. Each squeezer contains its own beauty and uniqueness. It got me thinking, why not dedicate this dessert to the tool that actually helps us every single time we want to make a lemon meringue tart?

I went ahead and bought a few lemon squeezers as I came to realise they are each so unique and beautiful as a stand-alone object. They all have a uniqueness in the design of the cone shape; some straight, some wavy, some small, some minimalist... but all designs serving the same purpose: squeezing juice.

In a way, they represent the negative space of a lemon and that thought is a beautiful beginning of a concept. Moving forward, I know I am aiming for a very graphic dessert, and this is why the mood board is showcasing shapes and forms of lemon squeezers. Fun fact: creating this dessert was the triggering point to my lemon squeezer collection.

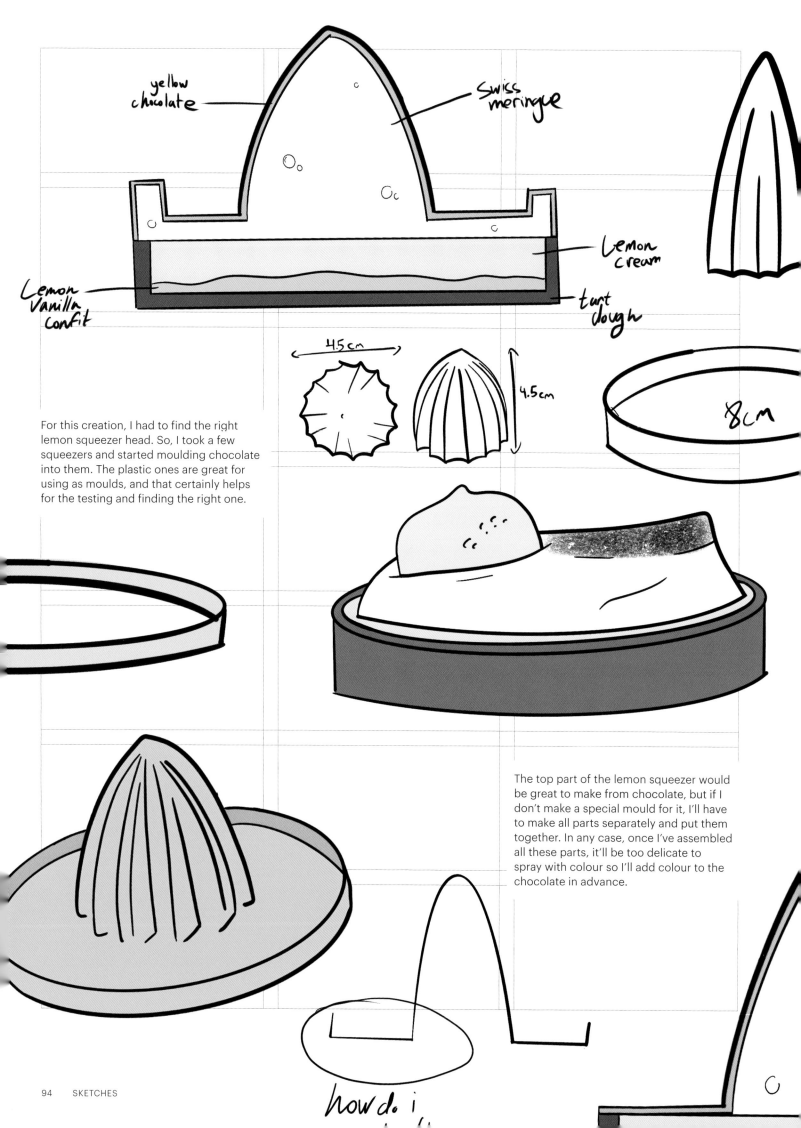

yellow
chocolate

Swiss
meringue

Lemon
cream

Lemon
Vanilla
confit

tart
dough

4.5 cm

4.5 cm

8 cm

For this creation, I had to find the right lemon squeezer head. So, I took a few squeezers and started moulding chocolate into them. The plastic ones are great for using as moulds, and that certainly helps for the testing and finding the right one.

The top part of the lemon squeezer would be great to make from chocolate, but if I don't make a special mould for it, I'll have to make all parts separately and put them together. In any case, once I've assembled all these parts, it'll be too delicate to spray with colour so I'll add colour to the chocolate in advance.

how do i

Parts?

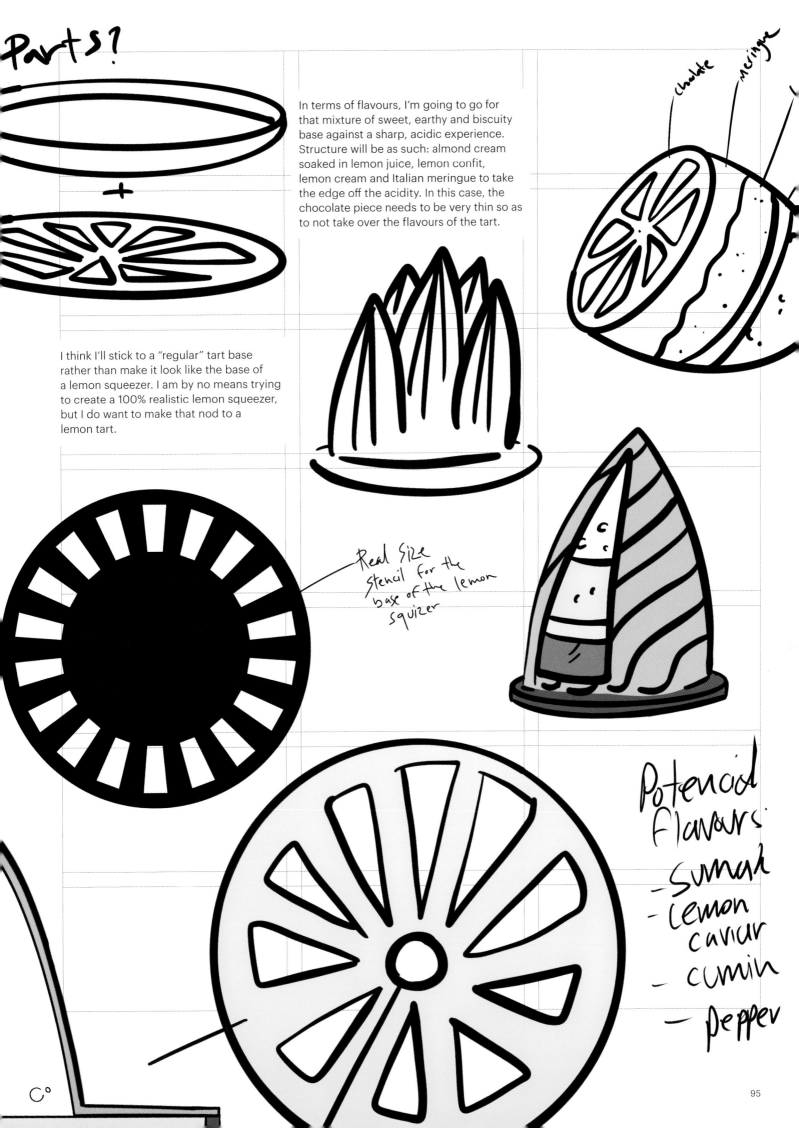

+

In terms of flavours, I'm going to go for that mixture of sweet, earthy and biscuity base against a sharp, acidic experience. Structure will be as such: almond cream soaked in lemon juice, lemon confit, lemon cream and Italian meringue to take the edge off the acidity. In this case, the chocolate piece needs to be very thin so as to not take over the flavours of the tart.

chocolate

meringue

I think I'll stick to a "regular" tart base rather than make it look like the base of a lemon squeezer. I am by no means trying to create a 100% realistic lemon squeezer, but I do want to make that nod to a lemon tart.

Real size stencil for the base of the lemon squizer

Potencial flavours:
- sumak
- lemon caviar
- cumin
- pepper

C°

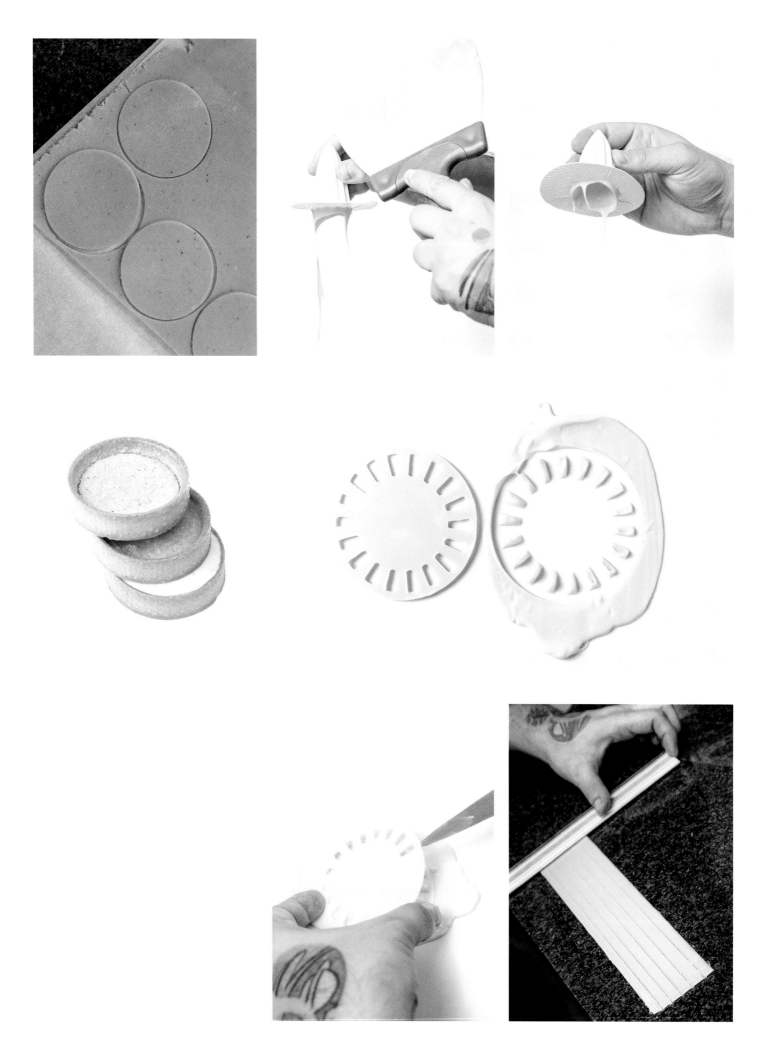

Sablé dough

400 g	flour
4 g	salt
90 g	almond powder
200 g	powdered sugar
250 g	butter
½	vanilla pod
90 g	eggs

In a stand mixer with the paddle attachment, mix the flour, salt, almond, sugar and butter. Mix well until a sandy texture forms. Slowly add the eggs and vanilla and mix until well combined.

Wrap the dough in cling film and cool overnight in the fridge. Roll the dough out to 2 mm thickness. Line the pre-greased tart rings (i used 8 cm diameter rings) and bake at 160°C for around 10 minutes or until it starts to golden (we will bake them again with the almond cream).

Almond cream

65 g	butter
55 g	sugar
70 g	almond powder
60 g	eggs
10 g	plain flour
½	vanilla pod
	lemon juice for brushing

In a stand mixer, with the paddle attachment, mix butter and sugar together until well-combined. Add the almond powder and mix again. Slowly add the eggs until the mixture becomes light in colour. Finally, add the flour and vanilla and gently mix until combined. Pipe around 10 g of almond cream into each of the pre-baked tart shells. Bake at 160°C for around 10 minutes.

Once baked, brush the almond cream with the lemon juice.

Lemon cream

28 g	gelatin
80 g	sugar (1)
5 g	lemon zest
140 g	lemon juice
210 g	eggs
100 g	sugar (2)
150 g	butter

In a saucepan, heat the sugar (1) together with the zest and lemon juice. In a separate bowl, mix sugar (2) and the eggs. Make a crème patissiere with the lemon mix (see page 7) and bring to boil. Remove from the heat and add the gelatin. Mix well.

Put through a sieve and let the preparation cool down for a few minutes. Finally, add the butter and mix with a hand blender to emulsion. Cover with cling film and let it cool and thicken in the fridge.

Italian meringue

60 g	water
150 g	sugar
60 g	egg whites

In a saucepan, heat the water and the sugar together. When the syrup reaches 112°C, using the whip attachment of a mixer, start whipping the egg whites.

Once the syrup is at 118°C, slowly add the syrup to the egg whites while still whipping, until a stiff peaks meringue forms.

Lemon vanilla confit

200 g	lemon juice
70 g	lemon peel
80 g	sugar
1	vanilla pod
3 g	pectin NH

Add the lemon peel to a saucepan of cold water and bring to a boil 6 times, changing the water every time.

Strain the water to only keep the lemon peels, and add to them the lemon juice and vanilla. Mix using a hand blender. Bring to a boil and cook on low heat for around 8–10 minutes.

Let the preparation cool to 50°C, then add the sugar and pectin and bring to the boil again. Let it cool completely.

Decoration and construction

Zéphyr™ 34% white chocolate
yellow colouring

In the baked tart shell, pipe a thin layer of lemon confit followed by them lemon cream up until it reaches the top edge of the shell.

Use the mould fabricated in a thermoforming machine (see page 7) to create the chocolate squeezer head.

Use the stencil made with the cutting printer (see page 7) to create the base of the lemon squeezer decoration (see sketches spread of the chapter). To do so, spread a thin layer of tempered yellow chocolate on the stencil and let it harden. Remove the stencil slowly.

Make a hole in the middle of newly created base, using a hot piping tip and stick the bottom of the lemon squeezer head to cover the hole. Pipe the meringue into the squeezer head through the hole and finally place the squeezer head over the lemon cream filled tart.

Make a 1 cm high yellow chocolate ring the same diameter as the tart and pass it on a hot surface for a second before sticking it to the top of the chocolate base previously placed on the tart.

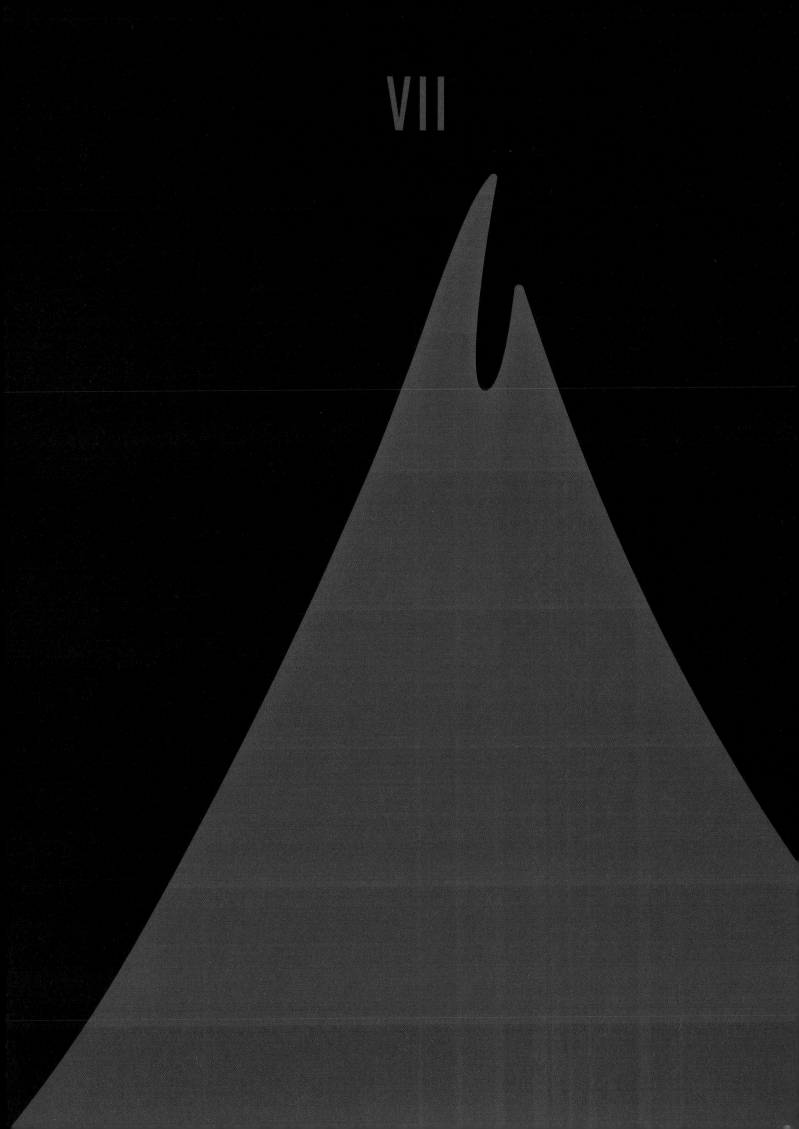

VII

VOLCANO

The idea of a two flavoured flan started cooking in my head a long time ago and I even tested it back in 2017, but in a more regular shape. I remember thinking, what would happen if a flan were to have more than one flavour? It worked pretty well once I found the right technique, but I put I put it to the back of my mind and didn't really think about it again... until now...

Volcanos are very intriguing, their structure and what it hides inside – that dangerous beauty, an enticing combination. That's why I enjoy watching videos of volcano eruptions – seeing the lava devour everything in its path, is as mesmerizing as it is terrifying.

Back in art school, we were studying Pompei and how it was all consumed by lava and ash, which somehow ended up preserving everything (including people) frozen in time. So when I started gathering ideas for this book, the first thing that came to mind when I considered volcanos was the 'surprise' element to their nature.

I understand that, on the outside, this flan will look pretty standard but what I love about this concept, is what it shares in common with a volcano: it's what it holds on the inside that will mesmerize you.

I'm thinking a lot of reds and black, as these are the two primary colours that come to mind when I think of a volcano or lava. I want this dessert to be "quiet" on the outside but unexpected once you get to inside, so I need to think about what will work well as an element of surprise. The mix of colours here will be used to emphasise the volcano, therefore I want to use activated charcoal in the dessert to create a realistic colour and feel. I will mix this with a strong shade of red – I am thinking raspberries. I want to capture an erupting volcano and use hard lava and flowing lava as a key part of my inspiration. I want people who cut into this dessert to actually see a volcano eruption.

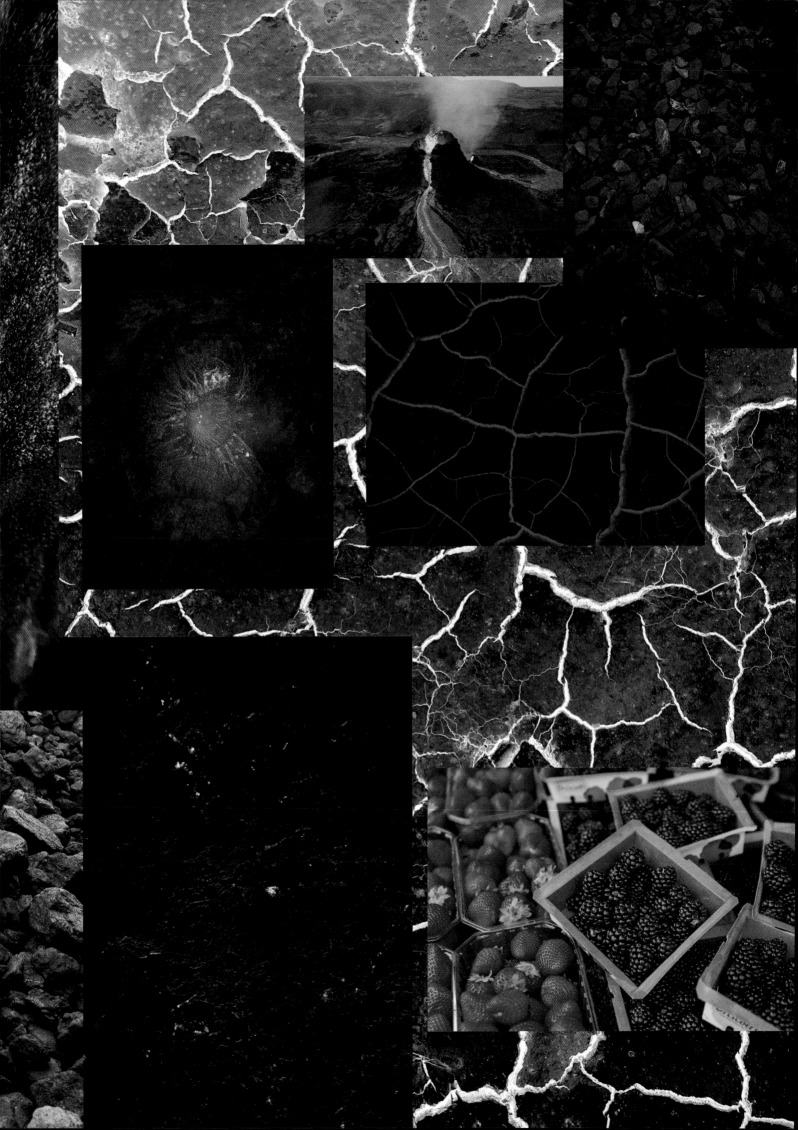

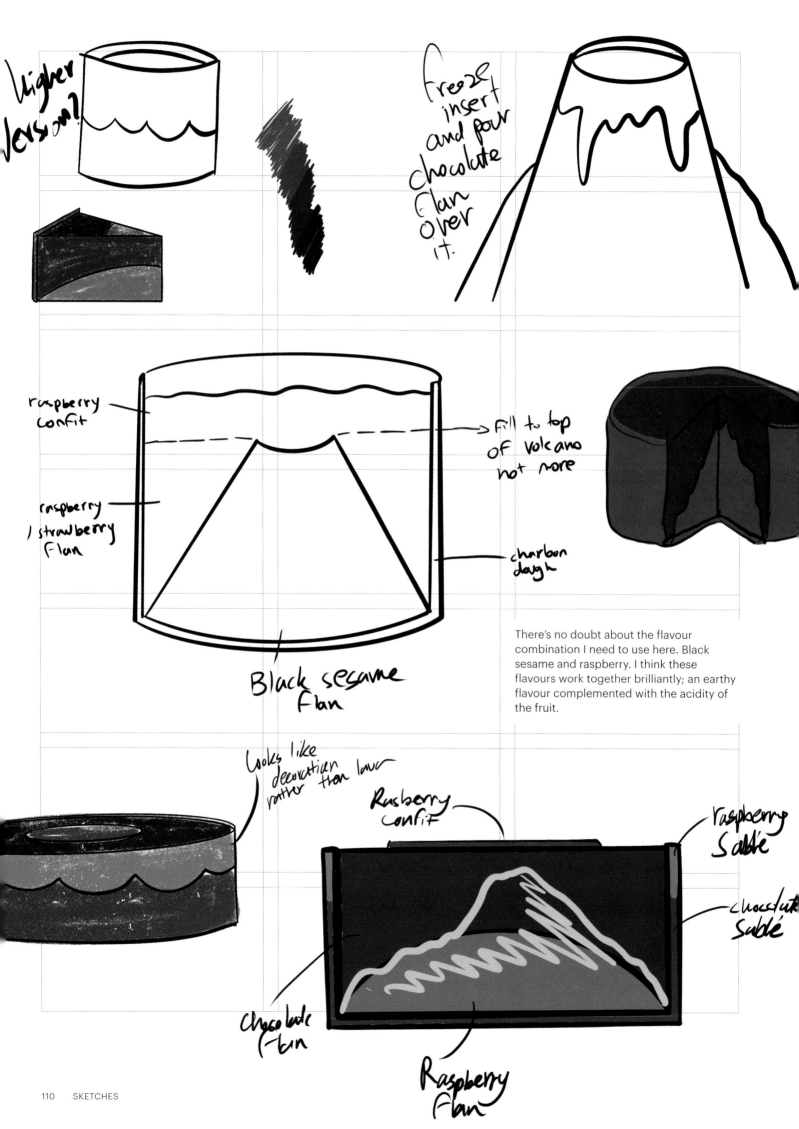

Higher version?

freeze insert and pour chocolate flan over it.

raspberry confit

raspberry / strawberry Flan

fill to top of volcano not more

charbon dough

Black sesame Flan

There's no doubt about the flavour combination I need to use here. Black sesame and raspberry. I think these flavours work together brilliantly; an earthy flavour complemented with the acidity of the fruit.

Looks like decoration rather than layer

Rasberry confit

Raspberry Sablé

chocolate Sablé

Chocolate Flan

Raspberry Flan

moule insert volcano

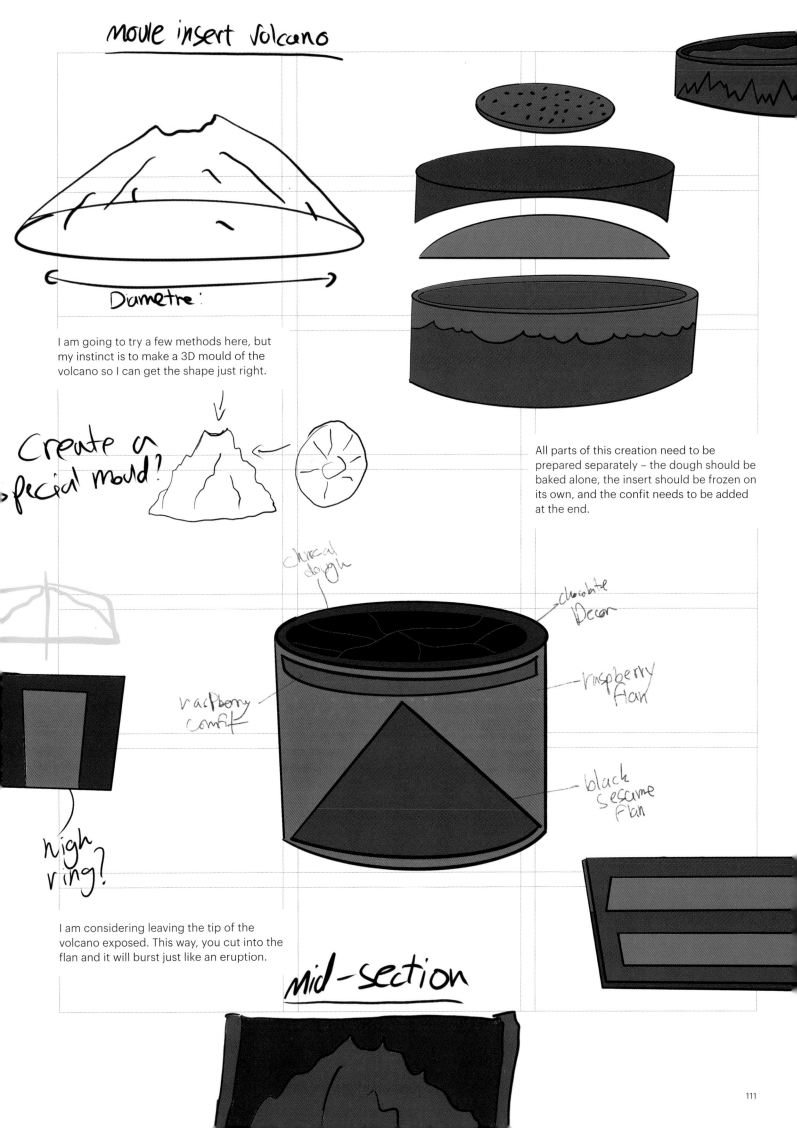

Diametre:

I am going to try a few methods here, but my instinct is to make a 3D mould of the volcano so I can get the shape just right.

Create a pecial mould?

All parts of this creation need to be prepared separately – the dough should be baked alone, the insert should be frozen on its own, and the confit needs to be added at the end.

charcoal dough

chocolate Decor

rasbberry comfit

raspberry flan

black sesame flan

high ring?

I am considering leaving the tip of the volcano exposed. This way, you cut into the flan and it will burst just like an eruption.

mid-section

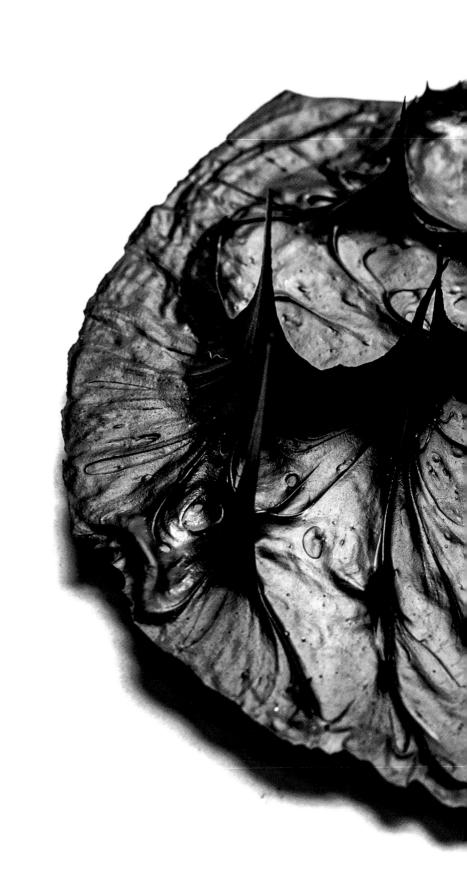

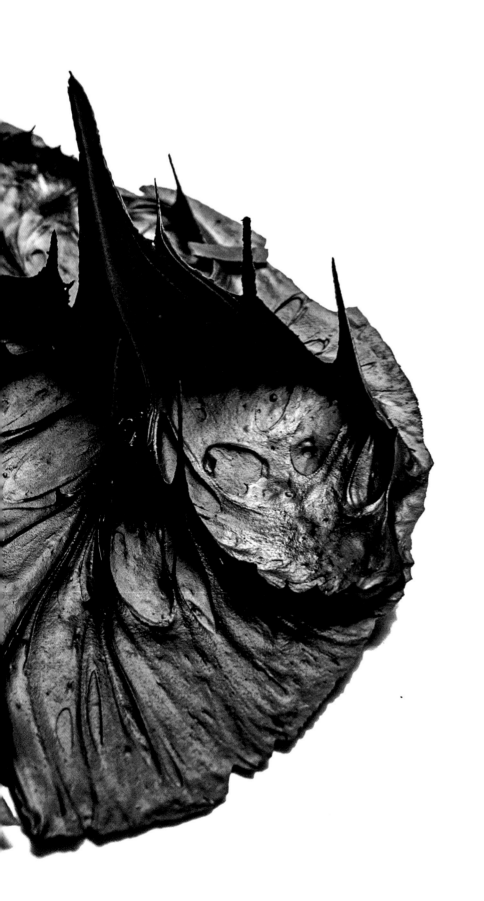

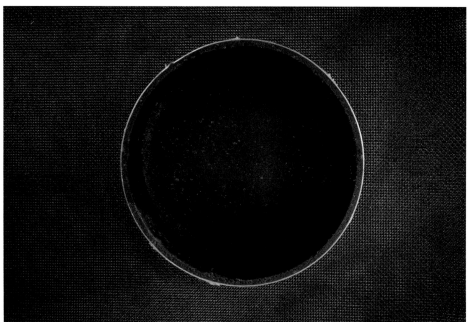

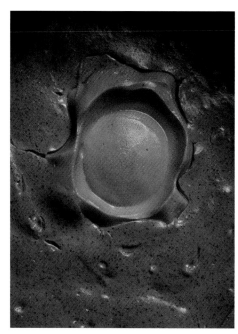

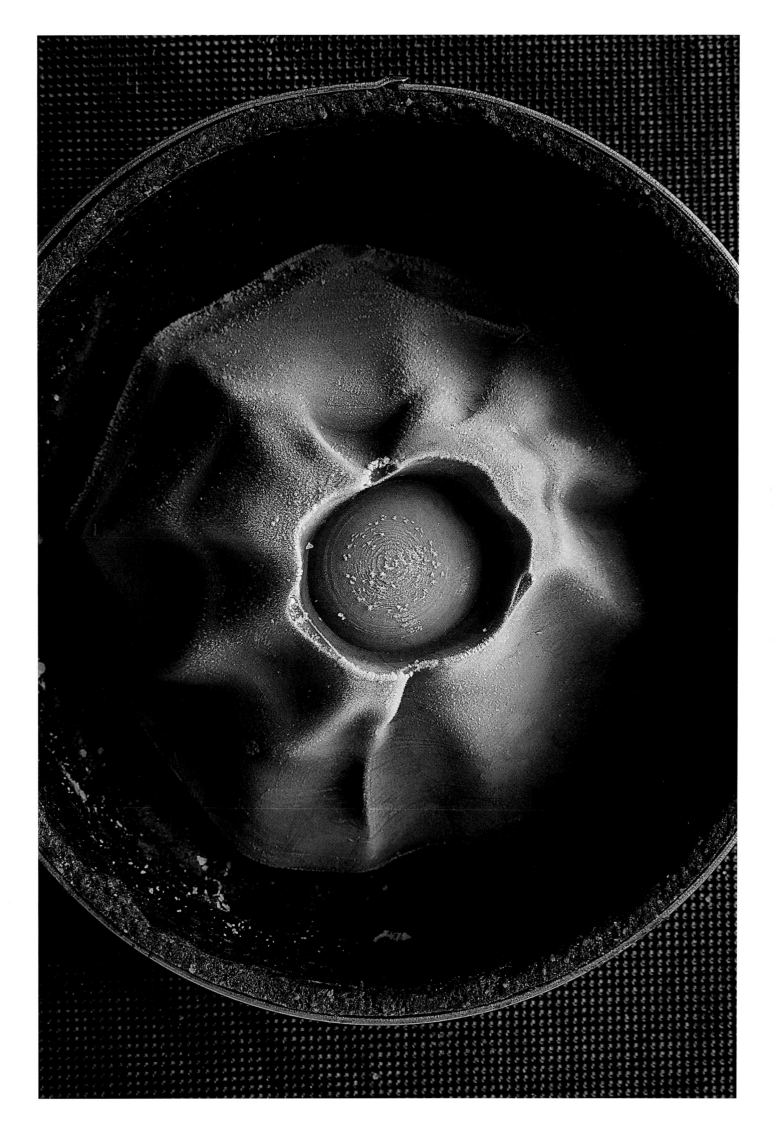

Black sesame tart dough

460 g	flour
4 g	salt
90 g	almond powder
200 g	icing sugar
210 g	cold butter
50 g	black sesame paste
90 g	eggs
7 g	activated carbon

In a stand mixer with the paddle attachment, mix the flour, the salt, the almond powder, the sugar, the activated carbon and the cold butter. Mix well until a sandy texture form. Slowly add the eggs and the sesame paste until combined. Cover in cling film and let it cool overnight in the fridge.

In a ring, line the dough at 3 mm thickness. Use a weight to blind bake the dough for about 30 minutes at 160°C.

Raspberry flan mix

160 g	raspberry purée
190 g	milk (1)
110 g	sugar
80 g	yolks
15 g	raspberry powder
30 g	cornflour
50 g	milk (2)
50 g	heavy cream
50 g	butter

In a saucepan, bring the raspberry purée and the milk (1) to a boil.

In a bowl, mix the yolks, the sugar and the cornflour and make a crème pâtissière (see page 7) with the raspberry mix.

With a hand blender mix the butter in the preparation, followed by the heavy cream and milk (2). Mix again and pour it into the volcano mould to freeze.

Black sesame flan mix

350 g	milk (1)
½	vanilla pod
50 g	black sesame paste
40 g	yolks
20 g	egg whites
45 g	sugar
30 g	cornflour
40 g	butter
50 g	heavy cream
50 g	milk (2)

In a saucepan, bring the sesame paste, the vanilla and the milk (1) to a boil. In a bowl, mix the yolks, the egg whites, the sugar and the cornflour and make a crème pâtissière (see page 7) with the sesame mix.

With a hand blender mix the butter in the preparation, followed by the heavy cream and milk (2). Mix again.

Raspberry confit

250 g	raspberry purée
200 g	fresh raspberries
75 g	sugar
4 g	pectin NH
15 g	lemon juice

Heat the raspberry purée and the fresh raspberries to 50°C.

Add the pectin and sugar previously mixed together and bring to a boil.

When it reaches a boil, remove from the heat and mix in the lemon juice.

Let it cool in the fridge.

Decoration and construction

Ocoa™ 70% dark Chocolate
black colouring

Remove the frozen raspberry flan mixture from the volcano mould and place on the black sesame baked dough.

Pipe the the black sesame flan over the volcano until it reaches the top of the volcano. Bake at 160°C for 40 minutes. Let cool completely then spread the confit over the top of the flan.

Temper the dark chocolate and the black colouring. Add a teaspoon of water and mix well.

Pour over a work surface and use a guitar sheet taped to the bottom of a tray to press down on the chocolate. Lift the tray in one motion. It's important to work fast here as the water crystallises the chocolate.

Let it harden without flipping the tray. Remove from the guitar sheet and place on top of the flan.

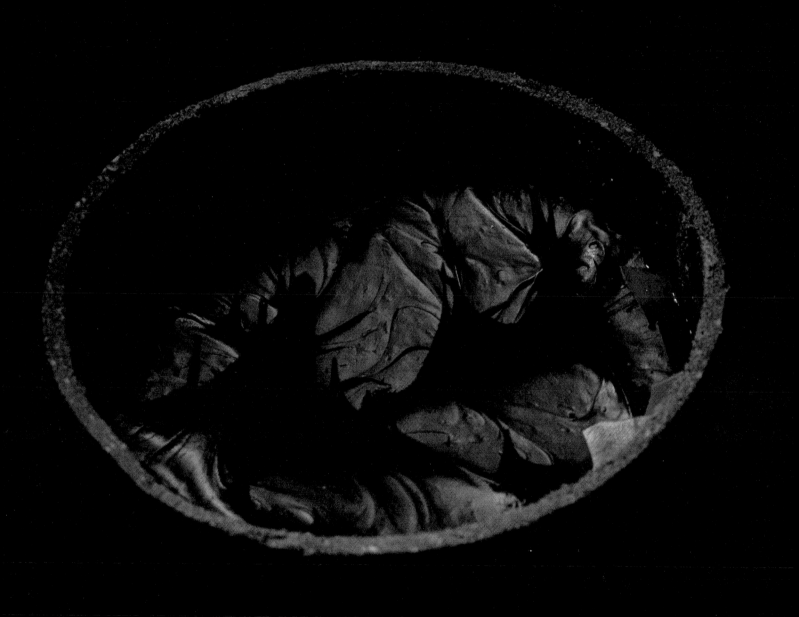

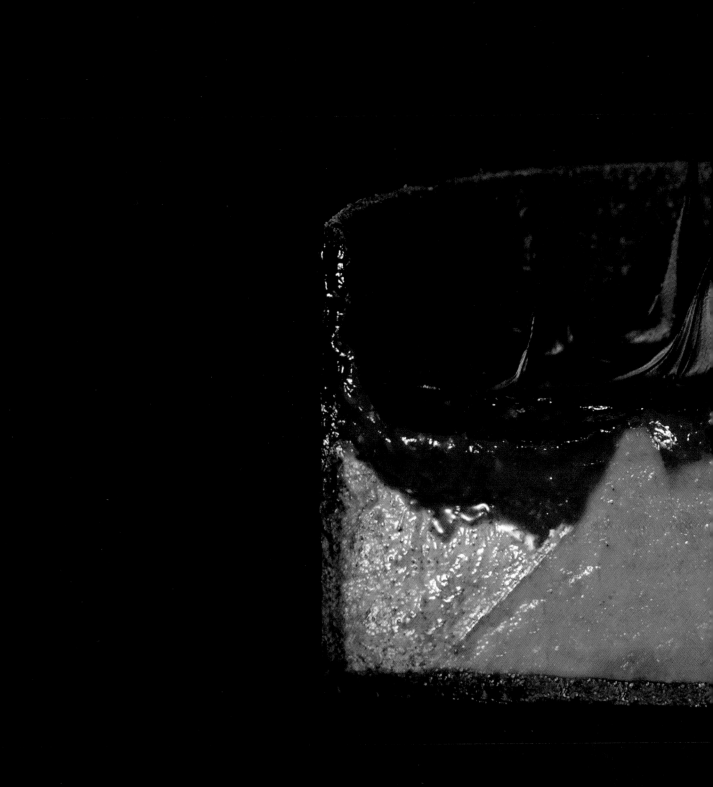

VIII

FORTUNE TELLER

As part of my curiosity about the unknown, I find fortune tellers intriguing, even though I won't go to one, simply because I'm afraid I'll have to suddenly live my life according to their instructions. I do find this world of communication and mysticism to be a huge source of inspiration, so when I started thinking about fortune tellers, I remembered being invited to a friend's house two years ago, while I was visiting Tel Aviv... needless to say, I was asked to bring the dessert. I wanted to bring a dessert that no one would expect in terms of flavours, so I decided to make one inspired by Turkish coffee. This isn't necessarily an ingredient one associates with desserts, which got me thinking about Turkish coffee readers: fortune tellers from a different school of thought.

So, I wanted to take all those flavours and the transportive element of the aromatic Turkish coffee (and the fortune tellers that do your reading whilst sipping on a cup) to create something of this mystical world. The blend of oriental spices and flavours is just the right combination for a well themed dessert. This will be my tribute to all of those flavours and will make you feel like you're in an old market somewhere in the Middle East face to face with a Turkish coffee reader, awaiting to hear what the future has in store for you...

PRESENT
NEAR FUTURE
FUTURE

PAST
NEAR FUTURE
FUTURE

DISTANT
FUTURE

NEAR FUTURE
FUTURE
PRESENT

FUTURE
NEAR FUTURE

PAST

ZOLTAR

SPEAKS

When I think of fortune tellers, one of the images that comes to mind is the classic: a mysterious person draped in exquisite cloths, decked out with golden jewellery, surrounded by a purple haze and staring into a crystal ball. With this recipe and creation, I want to show another type of fortune tellers, the Turkish coffee readers. I want you to feel the atmosphere that surrounds them with the first bite. The rustic and mystical charm of the scent of cardamom entering your nostrils. I love the idea of each coffee looking different when it is read, so I want to bring different kind of coffee stains to each cake. Making it your personal Turkish coffee dessert, by paralleling the work of a fortune teller.

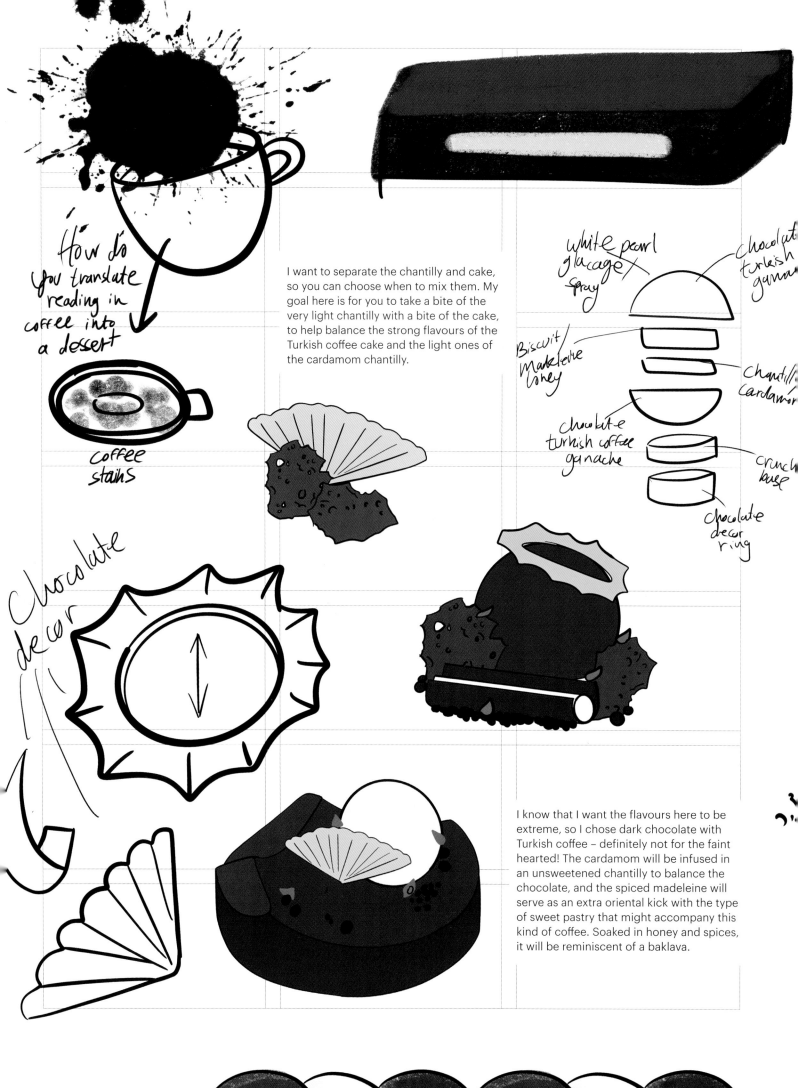

How do you translate reading in coffee into a dessert

coffee stains

Chocolate decor

I want to separate the chantilly and cake, so you can choose when to mix them. My goal here is for you to take a bite of the very light chantilly with a bite of the cake, to help balance the strong flavours of the Turkish coffee cake and the light ones of the cardamom chantilly.

white pearl glacage spray

chocolat turkish ganache

Biscuit/ Madeleine honey

Chantilly Cardamom

chocolate turkish coffee ganache

crunch base

chocolate decor ring

I know that I want the flavours here to be extreme, so I chose dark chocolate with Turkish coffee – definitely not for the faint hearted! The cardamom will be infused in an unsweetened chantilly to balance the chocolate, and the spiced madeleine will serve as an extra oriental kick with the type of sweet pastry that might accompany this kind of coffee. Soaked in honey and spices, it will be reminiscent of a baklava.

Each cake should have a unique pattern, kind of like the individual coffee stain you are left with when you finish drinking your Turkish coffee. I'm thinking of going with a white creation and splattering it with black – a different splash for each cake.

what if the cake looks like an espress cup?

I will try a chocolate technique that is achieved by creating a tube of chocolate to hold the chantilly. I want the chantilly to be separate from the cake and need to find the right creation to present it in.

Chantilly

chocolate tube with guitar sheet

2 cm   6 cm   2 cm

stick sides together

12 cm

cut   cut

chocolate decor

chantilly Cardamom

white spray

filo dough

chocolate turkish coffee cremeux

honey spices madeleine

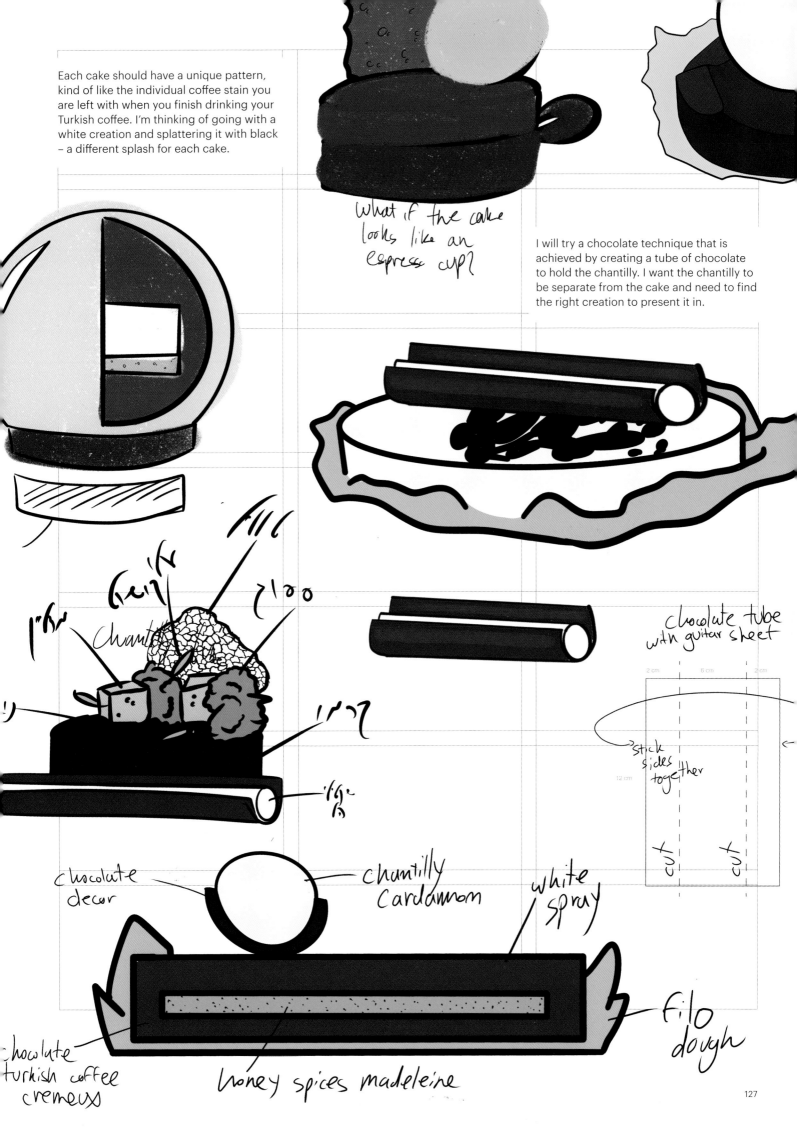

127

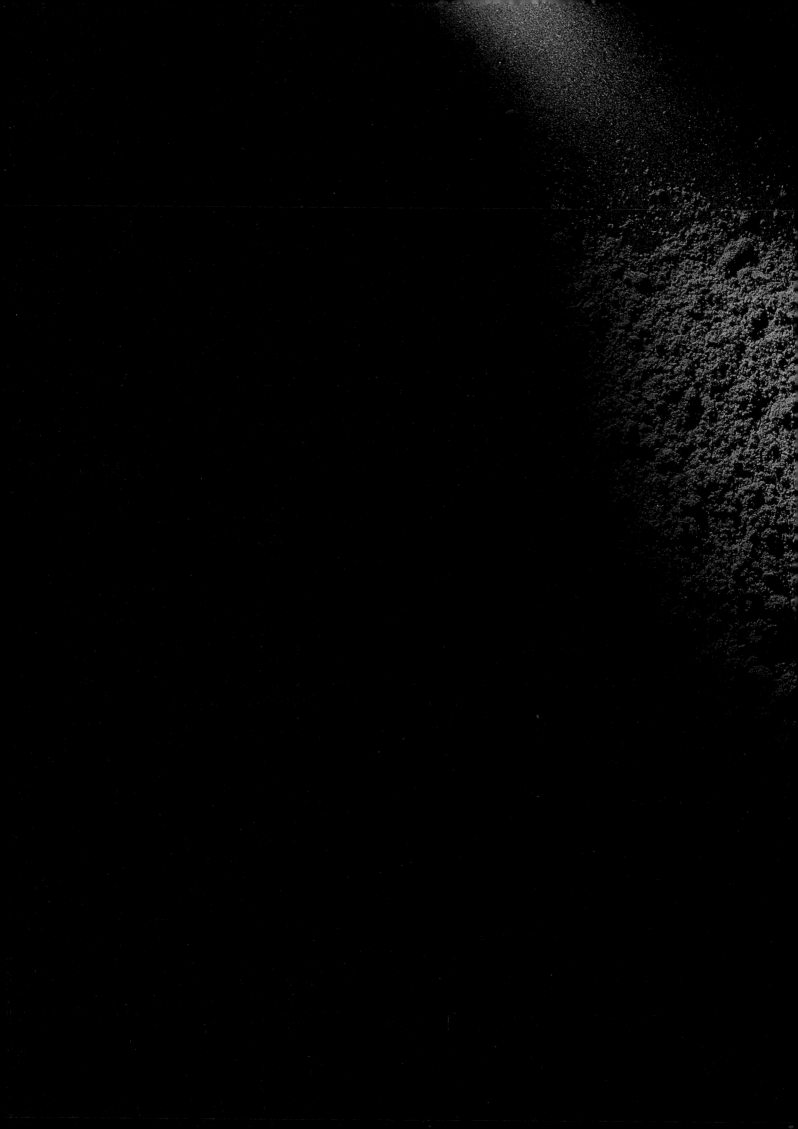

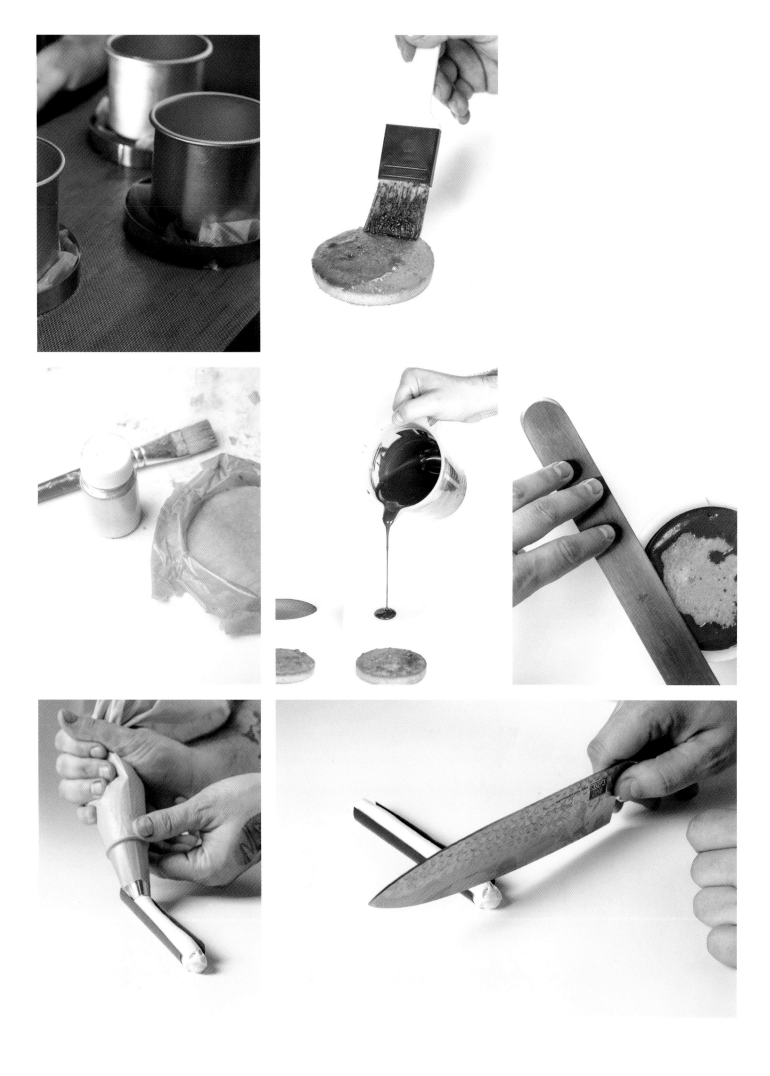

Chocolate Turkish coffee crémeux

140 g	milk
22 g	Turkish coffee powder
160 g	heavy cream
65 g	yolks
40 g	sugar
180 g	Saint-Domingue™ 70% dark chocolate
25 g	hazelnut praliné

In a saucepan, bring the milk, cream and coffee power to a boil. Remove from heat, cover with cling film and let it infuse for 30 minutes.

Strain the Turkish coffee to remove the powder and reheat the strained liquid to almost boil. Mix the yolks and sugar together and make a crème anglaise (see page 7) with the milk and coffee preparation. Use a sieve to pour the crème anglaise over the chocolate and praliné and mix well with a hand blender.

Honey Madeleine

100 g	sugar
30 g	honey
15 g	inverted sugar
140 g	yolks
140 g	flour
4 g	baking powder
140 g	melted butter

In a mixer, whip together the sugar, honey, inverted sugar and yolks. Sift the flour and baking powder and slowly add it to the mix. Next, add the melted butter slowly until well combined. Let this mixture cool overnight in the fridge. Bake in a size 8 ring, around 35 g of mixture per ring. Bake for 10–12 minutes at 190°C. Once baked, soak with the spiced syrup while still warm.

Spiced syrup

75 g	water
1 g	ground cinnamon
0.3 g	ground clove
35 g	honey

Bring all ingredients together to boil.

Cardamom chantilly

400 g	heavy cream
1 g	ground cardamom
42 g	gelatin mass
45 g	mascarpone
35 g	Zéphyr™ 34% white chocolate

In a saucepan, bring the cream and the cardamom to a boil. Remove from the heat, cover with plastic wrap and let it infuse for 20 minutes. Next, strain out the cardamom and reheat the cream until it is almost boiling. Remove from the heat, add the gelatin mass and mix. Once combined, pour the preparation over the chocolate and mascarpone and mix with a hand blender. Let it cool in the fridge overnight before whipping.

White spray

80 g	Zéphyr™ 34% white chocolate
100 g	cacao butter
	white colouring

Melt the cacao butter and the white chocolate to 34°C. Add the colouring and mix with a hand blender before spraying with spray gun.

Coffee stains

5 g	black and brown colouring
100 g	cacao butter

Melt the cacao butter to around 50°C, add colourings and mix with a hand blender. Temper to 27°C in a bowl. Using a spoon, take some of the preparation and splash over the cake.

Decoration and construction

olive oil
Saint-Domingue™ 70% dark chocolate
filo dough sheets

Spray olive oil over 1 sheet of filo and place a ring, the same size as the cake mould, on top of it. Place another bigger ring around the smaller one and fold the edge of the dough between the 2 rings (see photos in the making off spread of the chapter). Once done, bake for 10 minutes at 190°C or until golden.

In a mould, pipe the chocolate crémeux, place the honey Madeleine inside the crémeux and freeze.

Once frozen, spray the cake with white spray and splash it with some dark chocolate to make the 'coffee stains'.

Cut a guitar sheet 12 cm by 8 cm and spread tempered dark chocolate on top. Once the chocolate starts to set, cut 1 cm on the left and right of the chocolate (long sides) but do not remove the cut-out part from the guitar sheet.

Fold the guitar sheet together in the shape of a drop and stick the top together with a piece of tape.

Once harden, slowly remove the drop from the guitar sheet. Also remove the excess chocolate that you have marked on the left and right.

Carefully pipe the cardamum chantilly inside the chocolate tupe with a size 12 round piping tip. Take the cake, place it inside the filo dough and place the tube on top.

IX

CIRCUS

Full disclosure: I've never been a fan of circuses. The fact that I'm terrified of clowns doesn't help.

When I was a kid, I went to the circus and one of the clowns there took me to the centre stage to perform. I felt like everyone in the audience was laughing at me and not at the clown jokes. Talk about childhood trauma... I never went to the circus again!

However, I will say that, whilst there are many elements to circuses I find distasteful, there is something beautiful about the performance arts and the talents that execute them, especially in the field of acrobatics.

So, why a circus inspired dessert you ask? Because, alongside the performance art, I always enjoyed spotting a circus tent from afar. They're always huge and hypnotizing with their white and red colours. It's a joyful temporary structure, much like a dessert in a way.

Circuses bring to mind a sensory overload, particularly when it comes to the smells – caramel and popcorn and cotton candy. Even though I am not a fan of what goes on in the circus, I like what a circus represents: childhood, pleasure and sugar consumption.

It is for all these reasons that I decided to create a dessert dedicated to my perception of what a circus is... but from a distance.

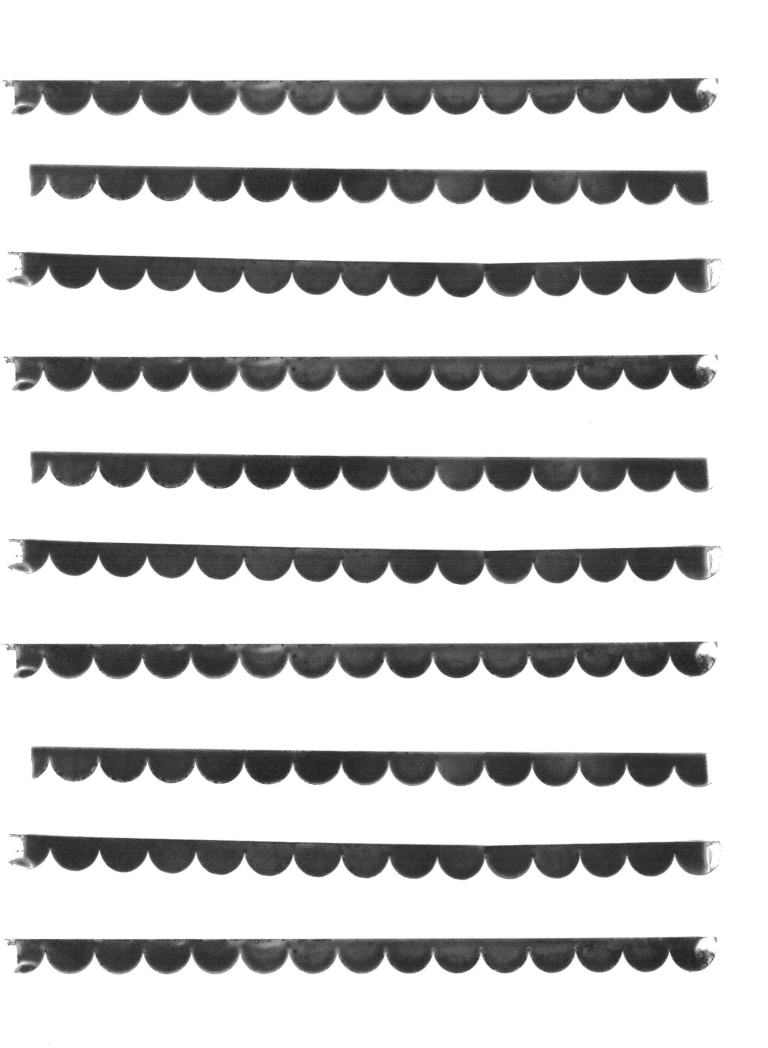

Circus tent, circus tent, circus tent... that's all I can think about. The red and white stripes, those huge ropes holding everything in place ,the flag on the top, calling out to the surrounding landscape: "were here!",. That's what I imagine a circus tent should look like. For this creation, I am focusing on reds and whites. I'm thinking of peanut, caramel and popcorn flavours, even marshmallow is a perfect possibility. Come to think of it, even the iconic popcorn box is made with stripes of red and white, resembling a circus tent. If I can put all of this into a design, the circus will be in town.

CIRCUS

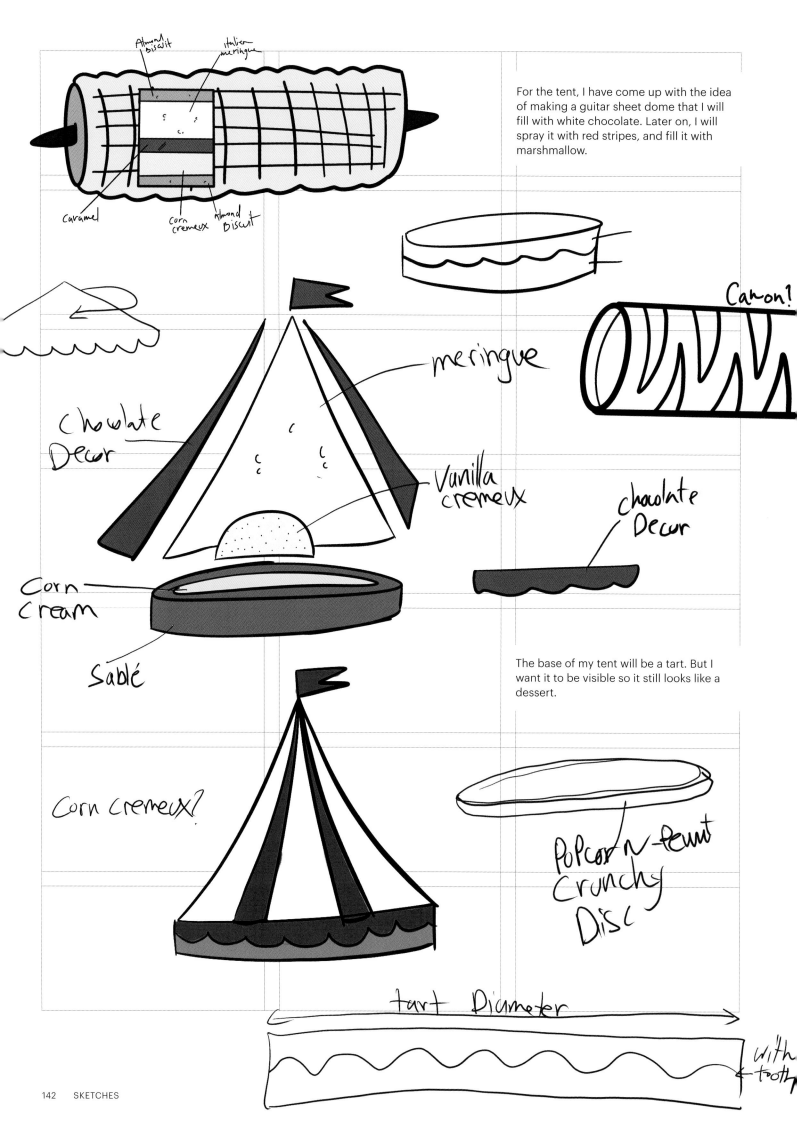

Almond biscuit

Italian meringue

Caramel

corn cremeux

Almond Biscuit

For the tent, I have come up with the idea of making a guitar sheet dome that I will fill with white chocolate. Later on, I will spray it with red stripes, and fill it with marshmallow.

Canon?

meringue

Chocolate Decor

Vanilla cremeux

chocolate Decor

Corn Cream

Sablé

The base of my tent will be a tart. But I want it to be visible so it still looks like a dessert.

Corn cremeux?

Popcorn-Peanut Crunchy Disc

tart Diameter

with tooth

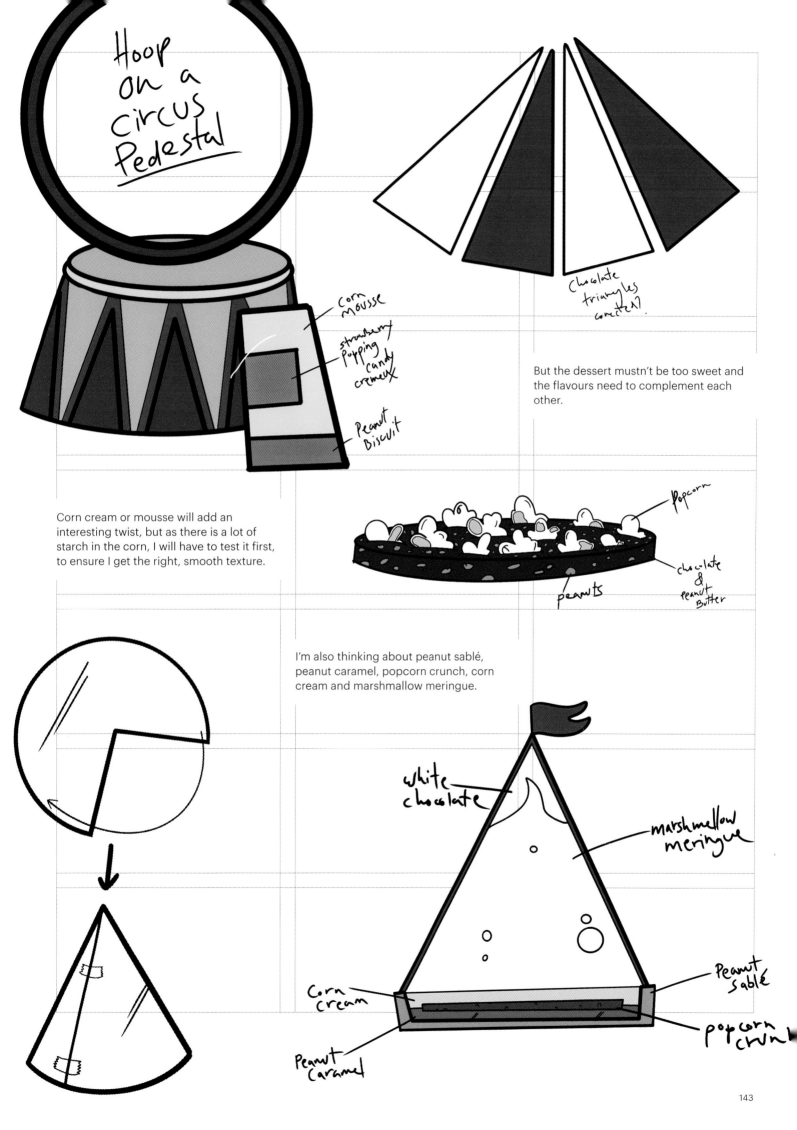

Hoop on a circus Pedestal

corn mousse

strawberry popping candy cremeux

Peanut Biscuit

Chocolate triangles corrected?

But the dessert mustn't be too sweet and the flavours need to complement each other.

Corn cream or mousse will add an interesting twist, but as there is a lot of starch in the corn, I will have to test it first, to ensure I get the right, smooth texture.

popcorn

peanuts

chocolate & peanut butter

I'm also thinking about peanut sablé, peanut caramel, popcorn crunch, corn cream and marshmallow meringue.

white chocolate

marshmallow meringue

corn cream

Peanut caramel

Peanut sablé

popcorn crunk

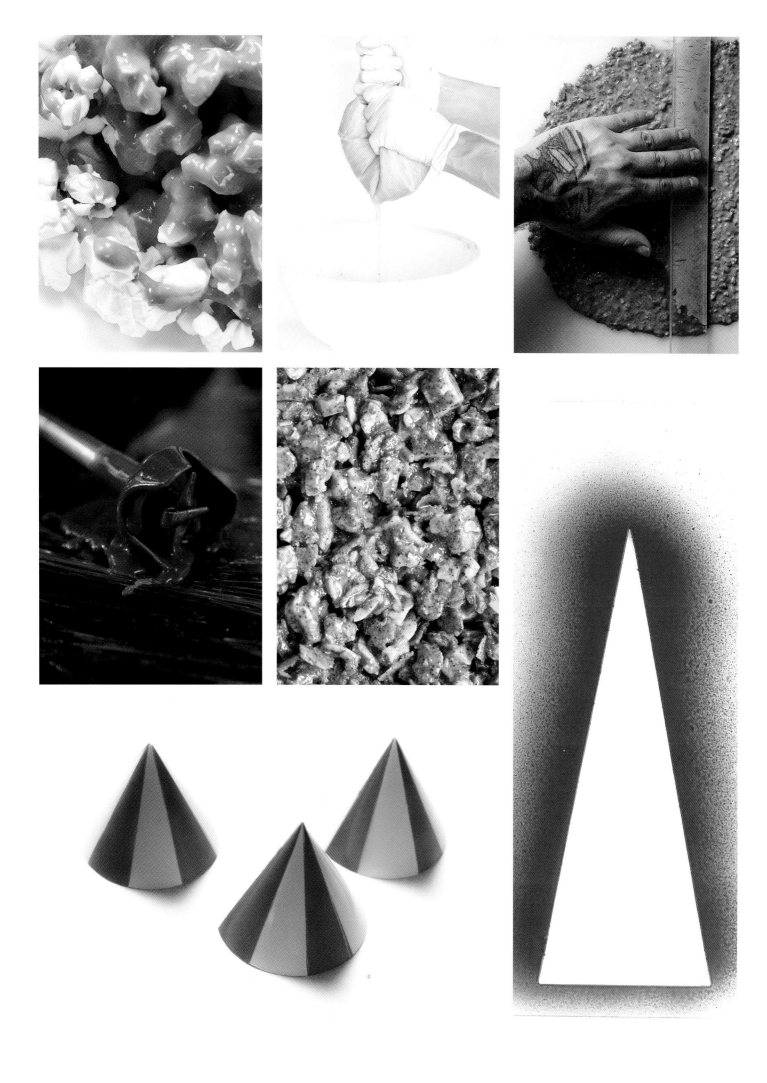

Peanut tart dough

230 g	flour
2 g	salt
85 g	ground peanuts
135 g	icing sugar
165 g	butter
½	vanilla pod
60 g	eggs

In a stand mixer with the paddle attachment, mix the flour, salt, peanuts, icing sugar, vanilla and butter until a sablé (sand-like) texture begins to form.

Finally, add the eggs in slowly and mix until combined.

Wrap the dough in cling film and let it set in the fridge overnight. To bake the dough, blind bake at 160°C for about 25 minutes or until golden.

Marshmallow meringue

40 g	water
100 g	inverted sugar
50 g	glucose
60 g	egg whites
24 g	gelatin mass

In a saucepan, bring the water, inverted sugar and glucose to 118°C. In a stand mixer whip the egg whites using the whipping attachment, and slowly add the sugar syrup. Melt the gelatin mass in the microwave and add it slowly as well, continuing to whip the mix until firm.

Peanut caramel

40 g	glucose
250 g	sugar
80 g	peanut butter
100 g	heavy cream
170 g	butter

Melt the glucose and add the sugar a little at a time, until a caramel is formed. Heat the cream and peanut butter together in a separate pan, and add to the golden brown caramel. Mix well, remove from the heat and add the butter.

Mix with a hand blender and let it rest until cooled down.

Corn cream

220 g	sweet corn
150 g	heavy cream
60 g	milk
45 g	sugar
65 g	yolks
1	vanilla pod
28 g	gelatin mass
80 g	salted butter

In a pan, bring the sweet corn, milk and cream to a boil.

Next, strain through a fine sieve and bring it back to the heat.

In another bowl, mix the sugar, yolks and vanilla and make a crème pâtissière (see page 7). Remove from the heat when it reaches a boil. Add the gelatin and combine. Add the butter and mix with the hand blender.

Popcorn disk

25 g	popcorn
50 g	peanut
50 g	feuilletine
115 g	Zéphyr™ caramel 35% chocolate
75 g	peanut butter
2 g	salt

In a food processor, blitz the popcorn, peanuts and feuilletine.

Melt the chocolate and combine with the peanut butter and salt.

Mix the 2 preparations together and spread a thick 2 mm layer over a silicone mat and cut out with a cookie cutter circles of 6 cm diameters. Let them cool in the fridge until solid.

Red spray for chocolate

100 g	cacao butter
5 g	red colouring

Melt the cacao butter, add the colour and mix well with a hand blender. Then temper to 27°C before use.

Decoration and construction

Zéphyr™ 34% white chocolate
red colouring
white colouring

Fill the shell with a layer of peanut caramel, followed by the popcorn disk and the corn cream on the top.

Using a guitar sheet, make a cone that is the same diameter as the shell of the tart. Fill the cone with the tempered white coloured chocolate. Remove the excess chocolate to create a thin layer and let it set. Remove the guitar sheet slowly and, using a stencil, spray with the red colour (see photo in the making off pages). Fill it with the meringue and place it over the tart.

Spread the tempered red coloured white chocolate over a guitar sheet. When the chocolate begins to set, using a toothpick, cut out a flag shape and let it rest.

Attach the chocolate flag on the top of the cone.

On an acetate strip, spread tempered red coloured white chocolate. When the chocolate begins to set, take the strip, and wrap it around a ring the size of the tart. Let it set until solid and place it around the tart.

X

ALIEN ABDUCTION

Full disclosure, I'm a huge sci-fi fan – UFOs and aliens in particular are my thing. Ever since I was a teenager watching The X-Files and walking back home at night terrified I might be abducted by aliens, I couldn't resist exploring this unknown world that also happens to tie in with my love for space. There's something so scary, yet fascinating about the potential existence of life on other planets. Being aware of the fact that we are not alone.

When I started thinking about the concept for this book, I knew I wanted to do something with a UFO. Including this fun tribute to my childhood (and current) interest was a must. However, I was afraid I'd end up creating a dessert that might be perceived as too childish. The pop culture world is fascinating, and I love being a part of that through my interest in sci-fi. Nonetheless, I always try to approach my creations with a certain level of sophistication so they can appeal to the young and the older (not old!) and even to those not interested in that particular sub-culture. So, here is my challenge: to create a homage to sci-fi culture that is mature but also a whole lot of fun.

Side note: I believe this is always a good thing to bear in mind while building a concept – how do you want your final result to be perceived?

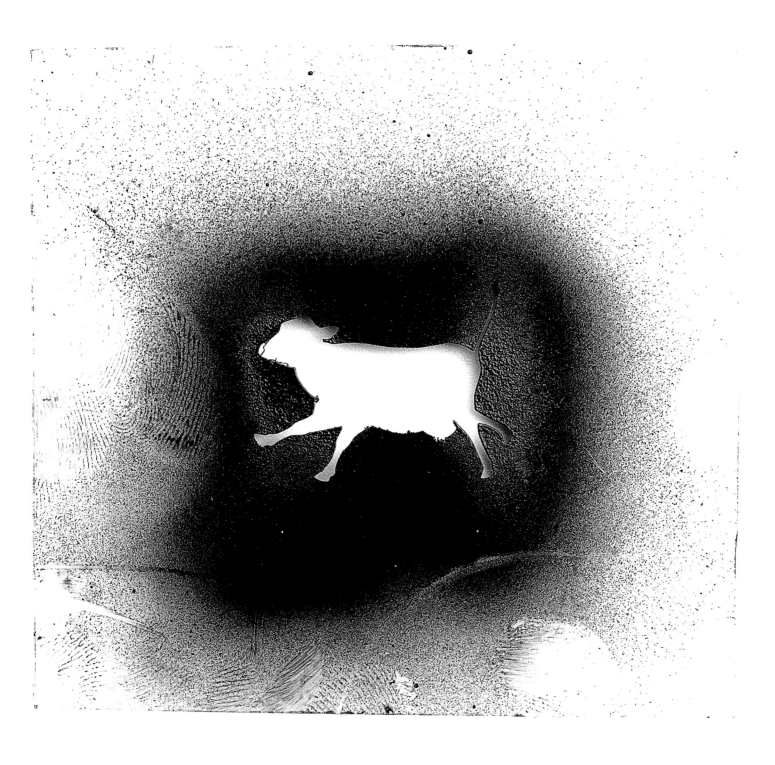

FLYING SAUCERS ATTACK!

EARTH VERSUS The FLYING SAUCERS

HUGH MARLOWE · JOAN TAYLOR WITH DONALD CURTIS

I WANT TO BELIEVE

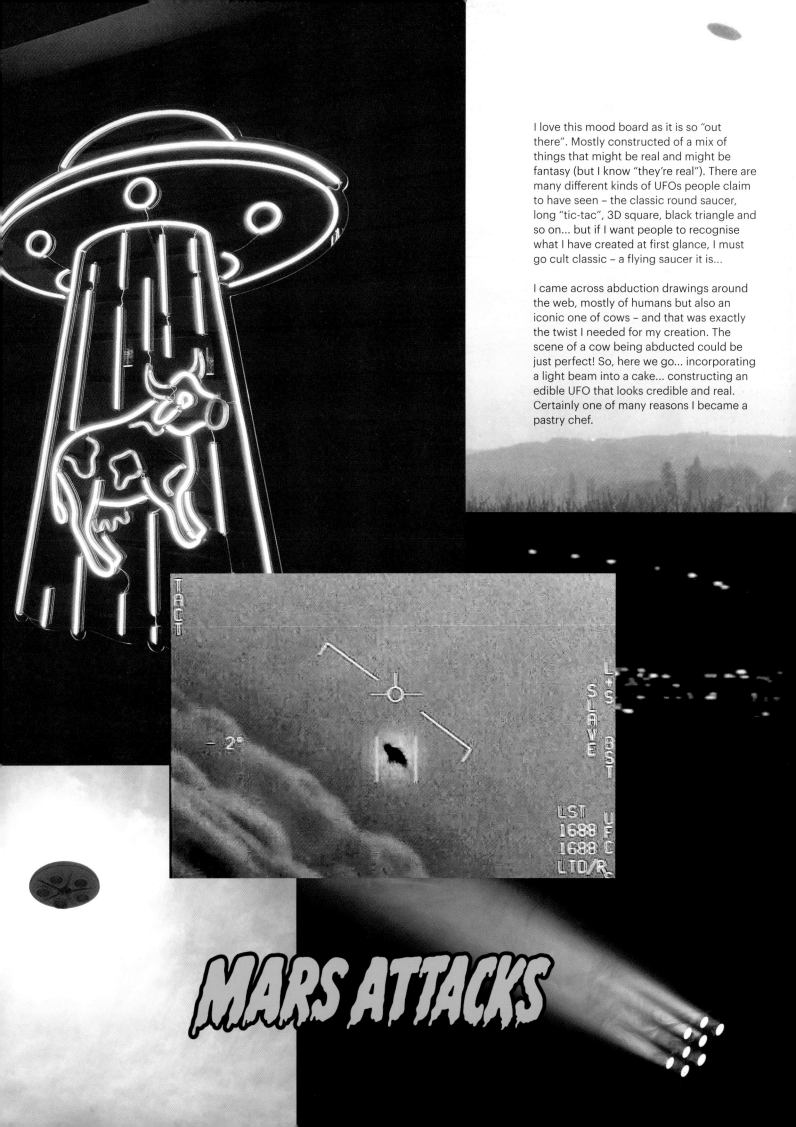

I love this mood board as it is so "out there". Mostly constructed of a mix of things that might be real and might be fantasy (but I know "they're real"). There are many different kinds of UFOs people claim to have seen – the classic round saucer, long "tic-tac", 3D square, black triangle and so on... but if I want people to recognise what I have created at first glance, I must go cult classic – a flying saucer it is...

I came across abduction drawings around the web, mostly of humans but also an iconic one of cows – and that was exactly the twist I needed for my creation. The scene of a cow being abducted could be just perfect! So, here we go... incorporating a light beam into a cake... constructing an edible UFO that looks credible and real. Certainly one of many reasons I became a pastry chef.

MARS ATTACKS

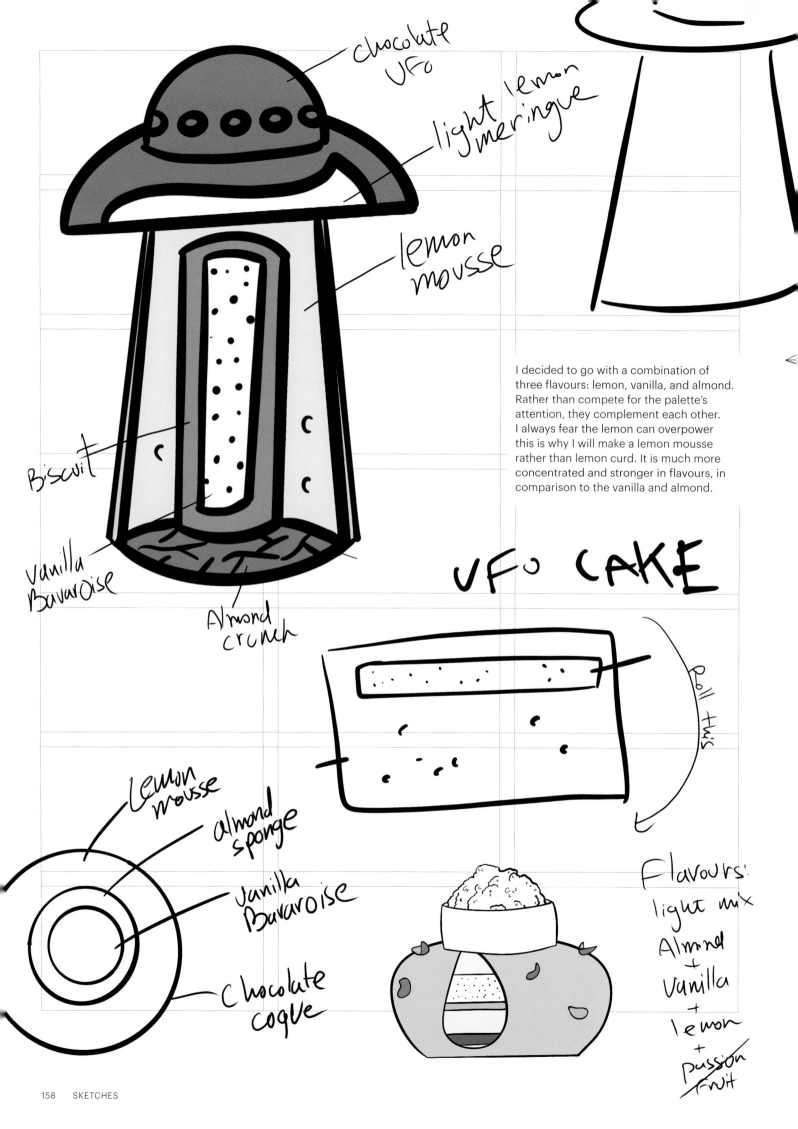

Chocolate
UFO

light lemon
meringue

lemon
mousse

Biscuit

Vanilla
Bavaroise

Almond
crunch

I decided to go with a combination of
three flavours: lemon, vanilla, and almond.
Rather than compete for the palette's
attention, they complement each other.
I always fear the lemon can overpower
this is why I will make a lemon mousse
rather than lemon curd. It is much more
concentrated and stronger in flavours, in
comparison to the vanilla and almond.

UFO CAKE

Roll this

Lemon
mousse

almond
sponge

vanilla
Bavaroise

Chocolate
coque

Flavours:
light mix
Almond
+
Vanilla
+
lemon
+
passion
fruit

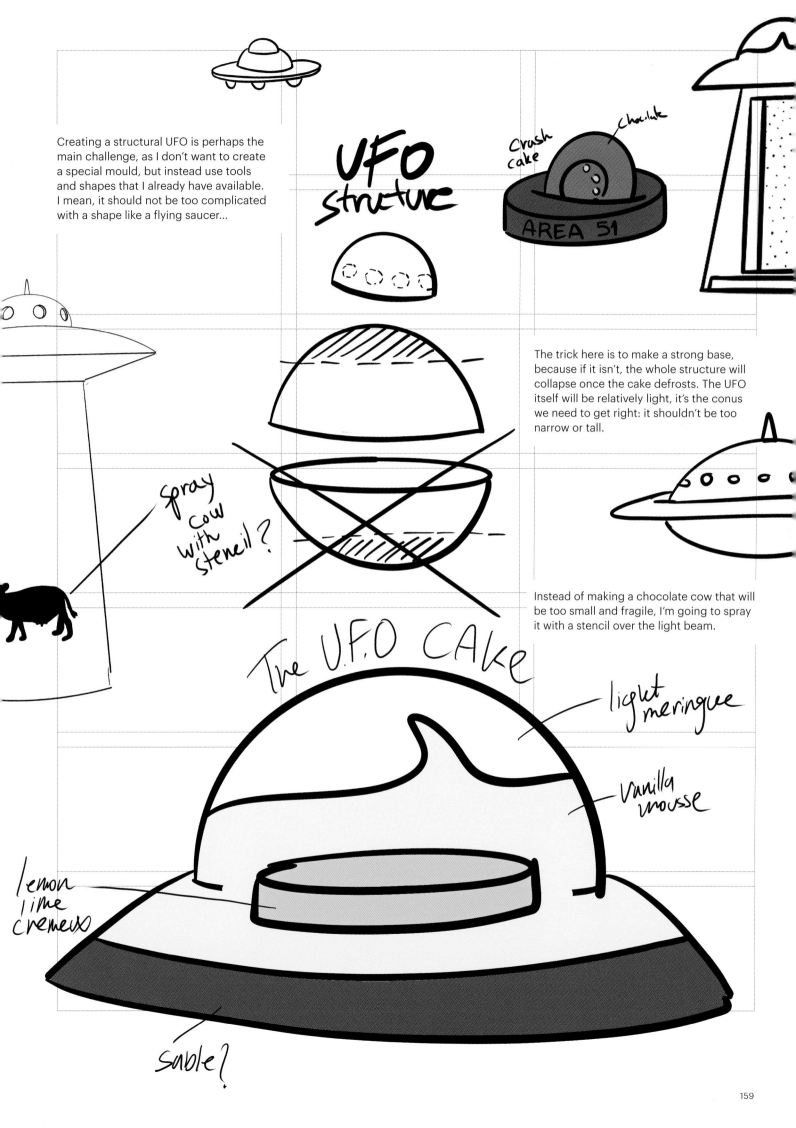

Creating a structural UFO is perhaps the main challenge, as I don't want to create a special mould, but instead use tools and shapes that I already have available. I mean, it should not be too complicated with a shape like a flying saucer...

UFO structure

Crash cake

Chocolate

AREA 51

The trick here is to make a strong base, because if it isn't, the whole structure will collapse once the cake defrosts. The UFO itself will be relatively light, it's the conus we need to get right: it shouldn't be too narrow or tall.

spray cow with stencil?

Instead of making a chocolate cow that will be too small and fragile, I'm going to spray it with a stencil over the light beam.

The U.F.O CAKE

light meringue

vanilla mousse

lemon lime cremeux

sable?

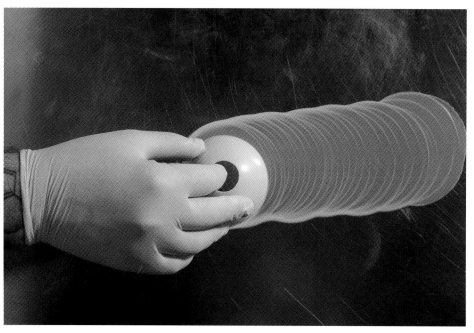

Almond Joconde

280 g	eggs
210 g	almond powder
80 g	icing sugar
40 g	inverted sugar
200 g	egg whites
85 g	sugar
100 g	flour
55 g	melted butter

In a stand mixer with the paddle attachment, mix the eggs, almond powder, inverted sugar and icing sugar. When the mixture is fully combined, take a small amount, add it to the melted butter and mix. Set this aside.

Next, whip the egg whites and sugar to soft peaks and fold it into the first egg mix. Add the flour and slowly fold in the butter mix.

In a 60 cm x 40 cm tray, bake at 240°C for 10–12 minutes or until golden.

Lemon meringue

40 g	water
40 g	lemon juice
6 g	gelatin mass
½	vanilla pod
75 g	egg whites
60 g	sugar

In a mixer, whip the egg whites with the sugar at medium speed. In a separate pan, heat the water and lemon juice to an almost boil. Remove from the heat and add the gelatin. Mix well.

When the mixture is at about 28°C, pour over the egg whites slowly and whip them together until you reach a firm consistency.

Vanilla bavaroise

21 g	gelatin mass
30 g	sugar
190 g	milk
70 g	yolks
1	vanilla pod
160 g	heavy cream

In a saucepan, bring the milk and vanilla to a boil. In a separate bowl, mix together the yolks and the sugar and make a crème anglaise (see page 7).

When this is ready, add the gelatin and mix well.

Let the preparation cool completely, then whip the heavy cream and fold it into the mixture.

Lemon mousse

150 g	lemon juice
125 g	sugar
100 g	eggs
55 g	yolks
28 g	gelatin mass
85 g	butter
275 g	heavy cream

In a saucepan, bring the lemon juice to a boil.

In a separate bowl, mix the yolks, eggs and sugar together and make a crème pâtissière (see page 7).

Strain and add the gelatin. Mix well. Add the butter and mix with a hand blender until combined. Let this mixture cool completely.

Once cool, whip the heavy cream and fold it into the lemon cream to form a mousse.

Almond syrup

100 g	water
40 g	sugar
5 drops	almond extract

Bring the water and sugar to a boil. Once ready, remove from the heat and add the almond extract.

Vanilla almond crunch

55 g	Zéphyr™ 34% white chocolate
85 g	almond paste
½	vanilla pod
20 g	chopped almonds
35 g	feuilletine
1 g	salt

Toast the almonds at 150°C until golden. Cool down and chop the almonds.

Melt the white chocolate. Once melted, add the almond paste and the vanilla and mix well. Add the chopped almonds, feuilletine and salt to the mixture and combine. Once ready, pour it into a ring so that the thickness is about 0.5 cm, Press down with a spoon and let it set.

Silver spray for chocolate

100 g	cacao butter
10 g	silver colouring

Melt the cacao butter, add the silver colouring and mix with a hand blender. Temper to around 27°C before use.

Use same recipe, using black colouring for black spray.

Yellow dipping glaze

500 g	Zéphyr™ 34% white chocolate
500 g	cacao butter
	yellow colouring

Melt the chocolate and cacao butter. Next, add the colouring and mix with a hand blender. Cool to 34°C before dipping the cake into the mix.

Decoration and construction

Zéphyr™ 34% white chocolate

Using a small half-sphere mould, make the chocolate spheres. Once set, remove the spheres from the moulds and carefully make a small hole using a hot piping tip (see photo in the making of spread of the recipe). Using a bigger half a sphere mould, make more domes. Reduce the bottom part of the big domes by half on a hot surface (see photo in the making of spread of the recipe).

Spread a thin layer of white chocolate on some guitar sheet and place the big domes on top. Let them cool until you can remove the domes along with the bottom part. Next, using a hot piping tip, make a small hole on the top of the dome.

Pipe the lemon meringue inside the big dome. Slide the small dome onto a hot surface to melt the edge slightly and stick it on top of the bigger dome.

Spray with the silver spray.

Make 2 cm diameter tubes using a guitar sheet (see sketches spread in the recipe chapter). Close one end with cling film and tape. Pour the vanilla bavaroise inside and freeze. Next, cut the joconde in a rectangle large enough to wrap around a tube ((also see sketches spread in the recipe chapter) and brush it with the syrup. Roll the joconde around the frozen tube of vanilla bavaroise. Cover in cling film and freeze.

Pipe the lemon mousse into a cone (see sketches spread in the recipe chapter) and place inside the bavaroise roll insert. Top with the vanilla almond crunch. Freeze. Remove the guitar sheet and dip the cone in the yellow dipping glaze.

Stick the chocolate UFO on top of the cake using some chocolate.

Use black colouring to spray the cow on the cone with a stencil.

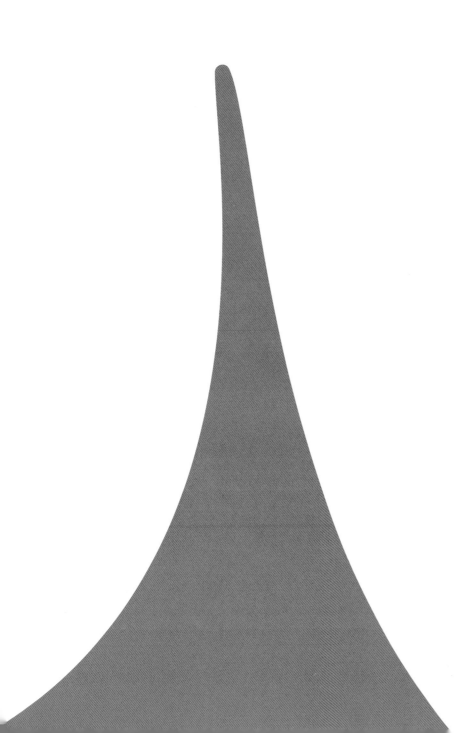

XI

MALABI

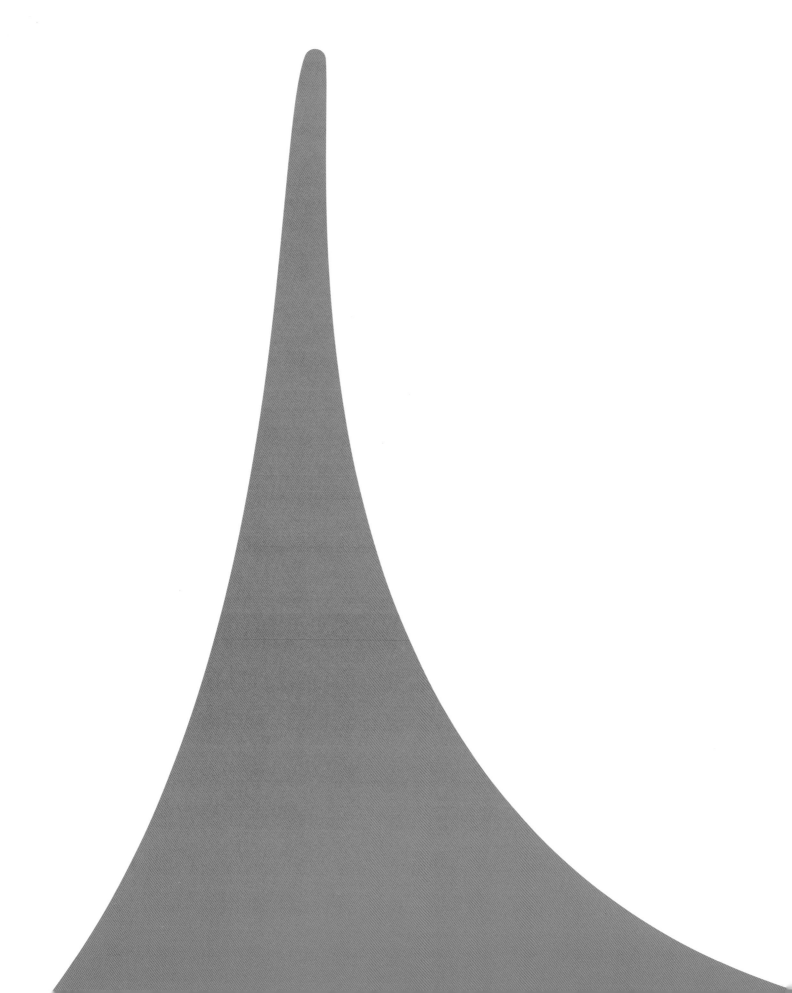

It felt very natural for me to make a macaron recipe for this book as I've been making them for years and years and years. I find joy in experimenting with different flavours and textures, and I've been doing it for so long now that I have been trying to upgrade this classic from the standard ganache and macaron shell to something new. And so, I came up with the idea of making a jelly macaron. This was mainly inspired by the idea of using jelly to prevent the ganache from spilling from the sides when you take a bite. And besides, I also wanted to add a new, fresh twist to that classic bite. That's when I figured I could mix two desserts I love into one. Running with these components, I started developing a new recipe for the macaron, containing a jelly and confit filling.

I wanted to connect this new recipe to my Mediterranean roots, and look to a dessert from my childhood to achieve the freshness I was looking for. It's called "Malabi" and it's a pudding-like dessert made with cream and starch, topped with rose and grenadine sauce, sprinkled with coconut, pistachios and peanuts. If I can translate these summery elements of the Malabi into a jelly macaron, I will be able to find that perfect blend between a French and a Mediterranean dessert.

Growing up Malabi was a summer dessert due to its light texture. Its wonderful combination of ingredients is a great inspiration for this creation that will bring a different 'bite' and new flavours to the traditional macaron we all know.

Here, my mood board represents the combination of two desserts. It's a dessert made up of two halves, one that feels very summer orientated, and the other, a French classic. I'm drawing my inspiration from the Malabi and implicating it into the macaron. The flavours are light – coconut, rose, raspberry – with a complementary colour scheme of white and red. Through trial and error, I have found a way of bringing together all these components – this is not only the job of a chef but also a graphic designer. Very conceptual, and very new. I'm taking my inspiration from the macarons I know and love, with classic flavours such as chocolate, vanilla, pistachio, caramel and so on... and I'm introducing them to the Malabi. While I still want to keep the look and feel of the macaron, I want to give it an element of tropical surprise upon the first bite.

MALABI

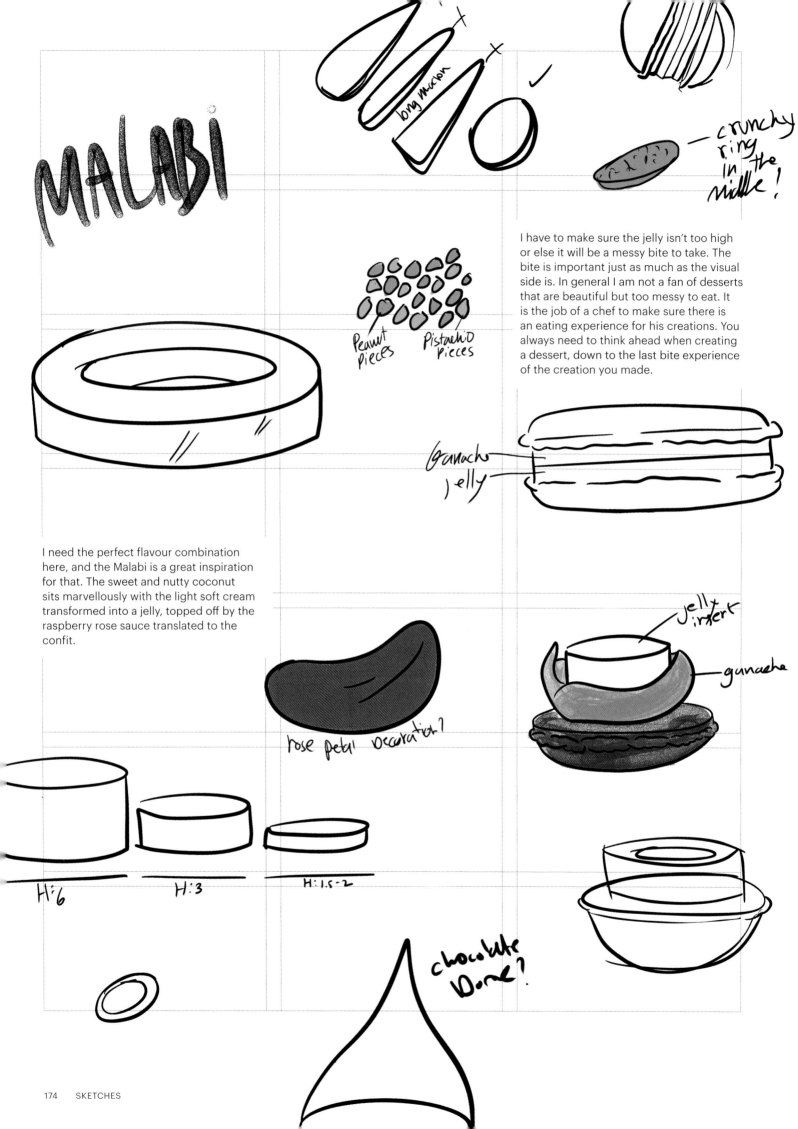

long macron

crunchy ring in the middle!

Peanut Pieces

Pistachio Pieces

I have to make sure the jelly isn't too high or else it will be a messy bite to take. The bite is important just as much as the visual side is. In general I am not a fan of desserts that are beautiful but too messy to eat. It is the job of a chef to make sure there is an eating experience for his creations. You always need to think ahead when creating a dessert, down to the last bite experience of the creation you made.

ganache
jelly

I need the perfect flavour combination here, and the Malabi is a great inspiration for that. The sweet and nutty coconut sits marvellously with the light soft cream transformed into a jelly, topped off by the raspberry rose sauce translated to the confit.

Jelly insert

ganache

rose petal decoration?

H:6   H:3   H:1.5-2

chocolate dome?

Malabi Macaron

Coconut – Rose
Peanut – raspberry

macaron

Jelly ring

ganache (montee?)

Macaron

Maybe confit in the middle and not ganache?
More Fresh!

The decoration on the top of the macaron will help to make that connection to the Malabi. That is a common touch in pastry, using decoration on the outside to hint on what is going on, on the inside.

Jelly ring

g

Jelly ring

g

MID SECTION

Possible SIZE: 4cm

Ro

Colors?
yellow/white
red/pink/purple

Ananas jelly ganach
Coconut jelly

Yellow macaron

Flowers — chocolat top?. **RUBY**

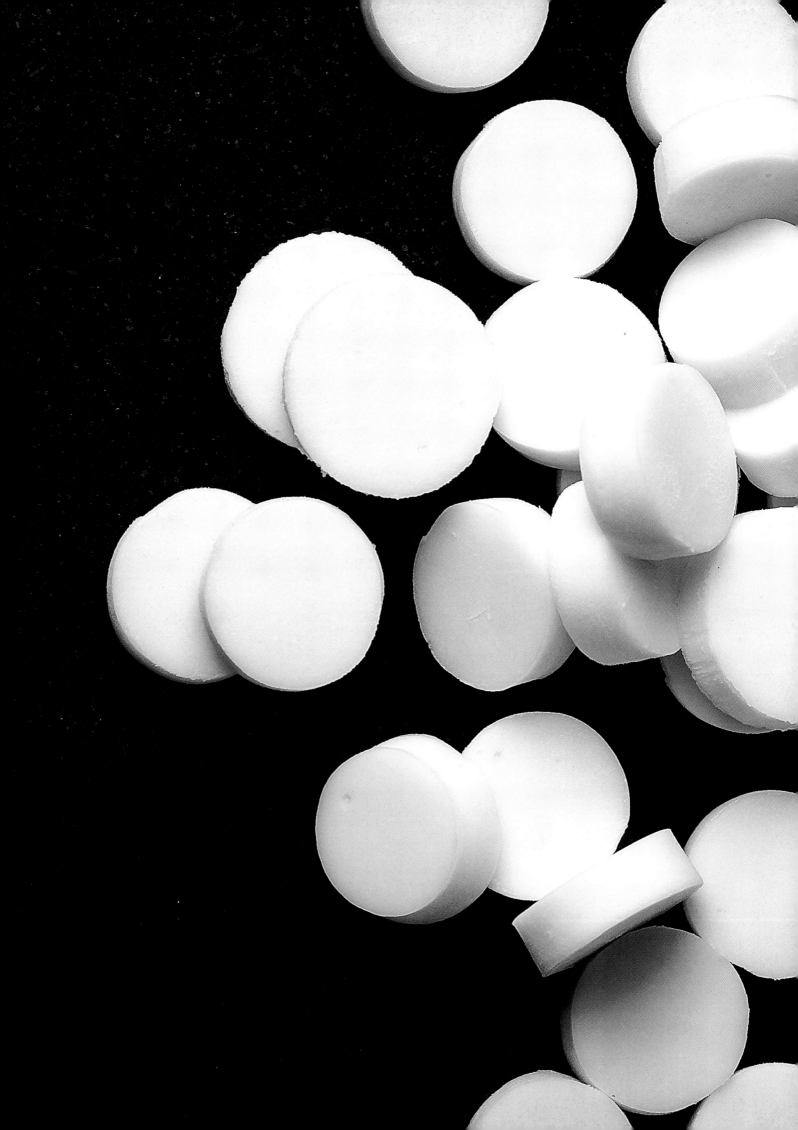

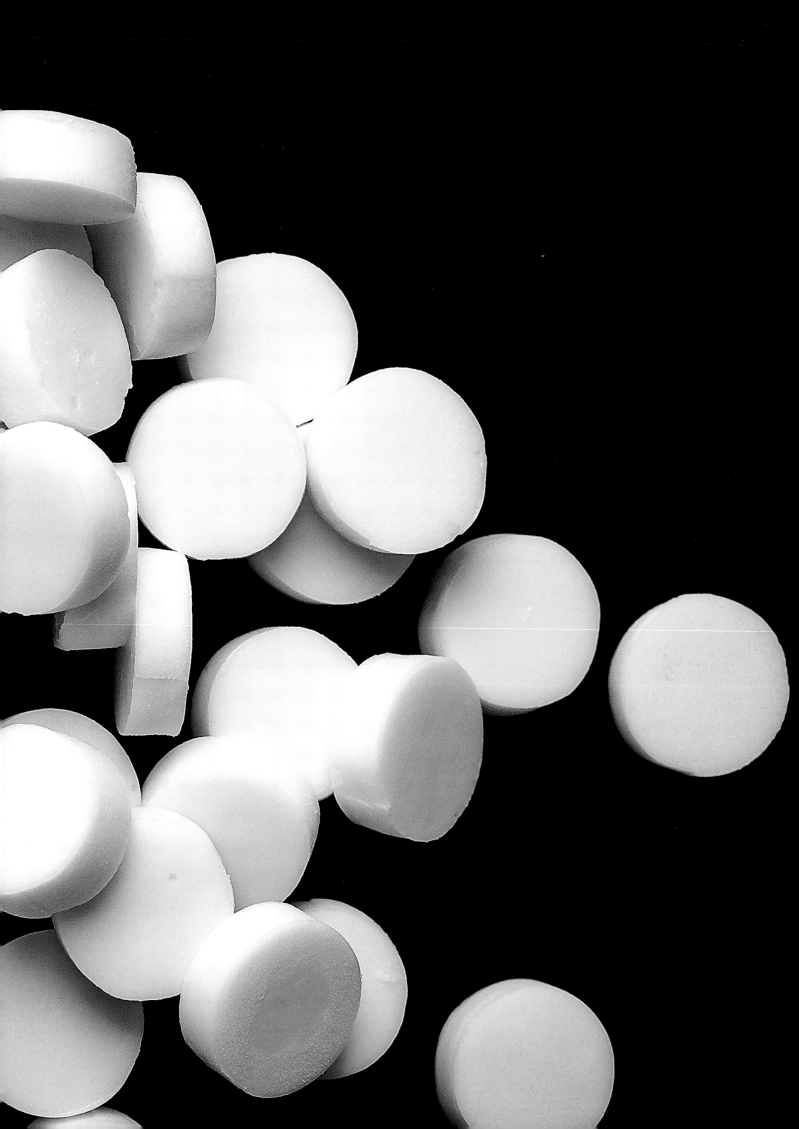

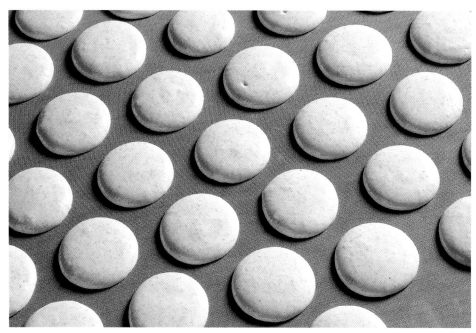

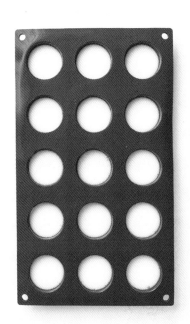

Macaron shells

250 g	icing sugar
250 g	almond powder
85 g	egg whites (1)
90 g	water
250 g	sugar
85 g	egg whites (2)

In a bowl, mix the icing sugar and almond powder together, add the egg whites (1) and mix.

In a saucepan, heat the water and the sugar together. When the syrup reaches 112°C, using the whipping attachment of a mixer, start whipping the egg whites (2).

Once the syrup is at 118°C, slowly add the syrup to the egg whites (2) while still whipping, until a stiff peaks meringue forms.

When both stages are completed, fold the almond mix into the meringue until well combined. Transfer to a piping bag with a 10 piping tip and pipe macarons onto a silicone mat. Let the preparation sit for around 15 minutes. Bake 10–12 minutes at 160°C or until dry.

Coconut jelly

200 g	coconut puree
200 g	coconut cream
60 g	glucose
8 g	yellow pectin
40 g	sugar
120 g	gelatin mass
20 g	lemon juice

In a saucepan, heat the coconut puree with the coconut cream and the glucose. When the preparation reaches 50°C, add the premixed sugar and yellow pectin while constantly mixing.

Bring to a boil for 2 minutes and then add the lemon juice and gelatin mass. Pour 1 cm high of the preparation into round moulds the same diameter as the macaron, and freeze.

Raspberry rose confit

150 g	raspberry puree
25 g	inverted sugar
14 g	rose extract
15 g	sugar
2 g	pectin NH
7 g	lemon juice

In a saucepan, heat the inverted sugar and the raspberry puree together with the rose extract to 50°C. Mix the sugar and pectin together and add it to the raspberry preparation while mixing and bring to a boil.

Once boiling point is reached, remove from the heat and add the lemon juice. Stir and let it cool completely.

Decoration and construction

Zéphyr™ 34% white chocolate
pink colouring
pistachio halves

Take half of the baked macaron shells, dip the round top of each in tempered pink chocolate and stick the shells from the flat side, using some tempered chocolate, to the bottom of a hanging tray covered with cling film. Let them set. Using a small round cookie cutter, make a hole in the jelly circles. Take the other half of the baked macarons and place the jelly rings on top of them. Fill the center of each ring with the raspberry rose confit and close the macarons with the chocolate covered shells. Decorate with pistachios.

XII

MÜLLER-BROCKMANN

This was an unusual choice for me. It might seem odd for me to pay tribute to a graphic designer, who worked in the 60s. Especially given that, as a former graphic designer, I was the complete opposite of Müller-Brockmann. His work is known across the world for his Gestalt when it comes to composition, typography and use of colour. His book *Grid Systems in Graphic Design* is considered to be a foremost authority in design and, we need to remember, that it was all done without the use of computers! In my Art Director days, my design methods were the completely opposite. While relying on the fundamental principles of graphic design, I was always trying to break the mould by using vivid colours, irrational typography and by forming uncomfortable compositions, at times making me feel like the design outcast at my university. But while we may be very different designers, I always felt inspired by his work and relied on his bases of grid and composition rules in my own. When I came across a series of posters Müller-Brockmann had created for the Zurich Concert Hall during my university days, I became fascinated by his interpretation of what the music would look like in a visual form. I was particularly entranced by the Beethoven poster, where one shape creates endless composition possibilities. From this point on, his work became my motivation as a designer. And despite an 80-year gap and very different methods, I knew something wonderful could be found in the process of this designer style-mashup.

musica viva

Josef Müller-Brockm

Grid systems

...raphic design

A visual communica...
for graphic designer...
typographers and
three dimensional de...

Raster syste...

...die
...elle Gestaltung

Ein Handbuch für
Grafiker, Typografen
Ausstellungsgestalte...

matthias hauer
werner speth
karlheinz stockhausen
jacques wildberger
igor strawinsky

végh-quartett...

paul hinde...
alba...
bé...

beethoven

tonhalle grosser saal
dienstag, den 22. februar 1955,
20.15 uhr
4. extrakonzert
der tonhalle-gesellschaft

leitung carl...
solist wolf...

beethoven ouve...
violi...
sieb...

vorverkauf tonh...
kuor...
kart...

musica viva

16. volkskonzert
tonhalle
grosser saal
dienstag,
26. märz 1957
20.15 uhr
tonhalle-gesell-
schaft zürich

leitung
hans rosbaud
solistinnen
yvonne loriod
klavier
jeanne loriod
onde martenot

o. messiaën
turangalila-sinfonie

vorverkauf
tonhalle hug jecklin
genossenschafts-
buchhandlung
karten fr.1.- bis 3.-

hans rosbaud
o. messiaën

I knew I wanted to go for a black and
white dessert. Sharp lines, almost as if
they were cut out with scissors, just like a
Müller-Brockmann design. I concentrated
on his graphic works for music posters,
and the emotions he was trying to convey
through his interpretation of sound. I am
fascinated with the true craftsmanship
and not the modern, automated mode of
output from a computer. I pride myself in
my work as a chef, which involves intricate
hand work that cannot be replaced by a
computer. Thinking of him cutting shapes
with scissors while I work chocolate with a
spatula – it's the kind of drive I need for this
creation.

19. volkskonzert der
tonhalle-gesellschaft
zürich
dienstag, 5. mai 1959
20.15 uhr
tonhalle großer saal

...sica viva
...leitung
hans rosbaud
...solist
wolfgang marschner

anton von webern
...echs orchester-
...tücke op. 6
...nzert op. 36

kleiner tonhallesaal donnerstag, 19. novem...

beethoven

Juni-Festwochen Zürich 1951
Tonhalle Grosser Saal
Dienstag, den 19. Juni 1951, 20.15 Uhr

C. M. v. Weber Ouvertüre zur Oper „Euryanthe"
F. Chopin Klavierkonzert Nr.1, in e-moll
P. Tschaikowsky Sinfonie Nr. 4, in f-moll, op. 36

Karten zu Fr. 5.50 bis 16.50 im Vorverkauf:
Tonhallekasse, Hug & Co., Jecklin und Kuoni

Samstag, 8. Juni 18.00 Uhr
Die Meistersinger von Nürnberg
Oper von Richard Wagner
Zum 150. Geburtstag
Richard Wagners
Richard Wagners
Sonntag, 9. Juni 20.00 Uhr
Die Zauberflöte
Oper von
Wolfgang Amadeus Mozart
Dienstag, 11. Juni 20.00 Uhr
Fidelio
Oper von
Ludwig van Beethoven
Freitag, 14. Juni 20.00 Uhr
Otello
Oper von Giuseppe Verdi

Samstag, 15. Juni 18.00 Uhr
Parsifal
Bühnenweihfestspiel von
Richard Wagner
Zum 150. Geburtstag
Richard Wagners
Mittwoch,19. Juni 20.00 Uhr
Il Trovatore
Oper von Giuseppe Verdi
Freitag, 21. Juni 20.00 Uhr
Rigoletto
Oper von Giuseppe Verdi

Sonntag, 23. Juni 20.00 Uhr
Mittwoch, 26. Juni 20.00 Uhr
Welturaufführung
Die Errettung Thebens
Oper von
Rudolf Kelterborn
Freitag, 28. Juni 20.00 Uhr
Samstag, 30. Juni 20.00 Uhr
London's Festival Ballet
1. Programm
Samstag, 29. Juni 20.00 Uhr
Sonntag, 30. Juni 14.30 Uhr
London's Festival Ballet
2. Programm

tonhalle grosser saal
dienstag, den 22 februar 1956,
20.15 uhr
4. extrakonzert
der tonhalle-gesellschaft

leitung carl schuricht
solist wolfgang schneiderhan

beethoven ouverture zu «coriolan», op. 62
violinkonzert in d-dur, op. 61
siebente sinfonie in a-dur, op. 92

vorverkauf tonhalle-kasse, hug, jecklin,
kuoni
karten, zu fr. 3.5- bis 8 50

Internationale
Juni-Festwochen
Stadttheater
Zürich
1963
tonhalle-orchester

karlheinz be grosser saal

musica viva

mar 1958 schweizerische erstaufführungen
hallesaal andré jolivet
cinque danses rituelles
ernst krenek
zweites klavierkonzert
luigi nono
«y su sangre va vienne cantando»
musik für flöte und kleines orchester
bernd aloys zimmermann
sinfonie in einem satz

karten fr. 1.- 2.- und 3.-
vorverkauf tonhallekasse hug
jecklin kuoni
genossenschaftsbuchhandlung

a viva

goffredo petrassi
schmid darius milhaud
eumeier paul hindemith
kertesz rolf liebermann

Anthologie
de musique
suisse

Un panorama
de la musique suisse
du 9ème siècle jusqu'à nos jours

Sur 50 disques
d'éminents artistes suisses
interprètent
257 œuvres de 142 compositeurs

Renseignements,
prospectus et vente
par votre marchand de disques

Communauté de travail
pour la diffusion
de la musique suisse

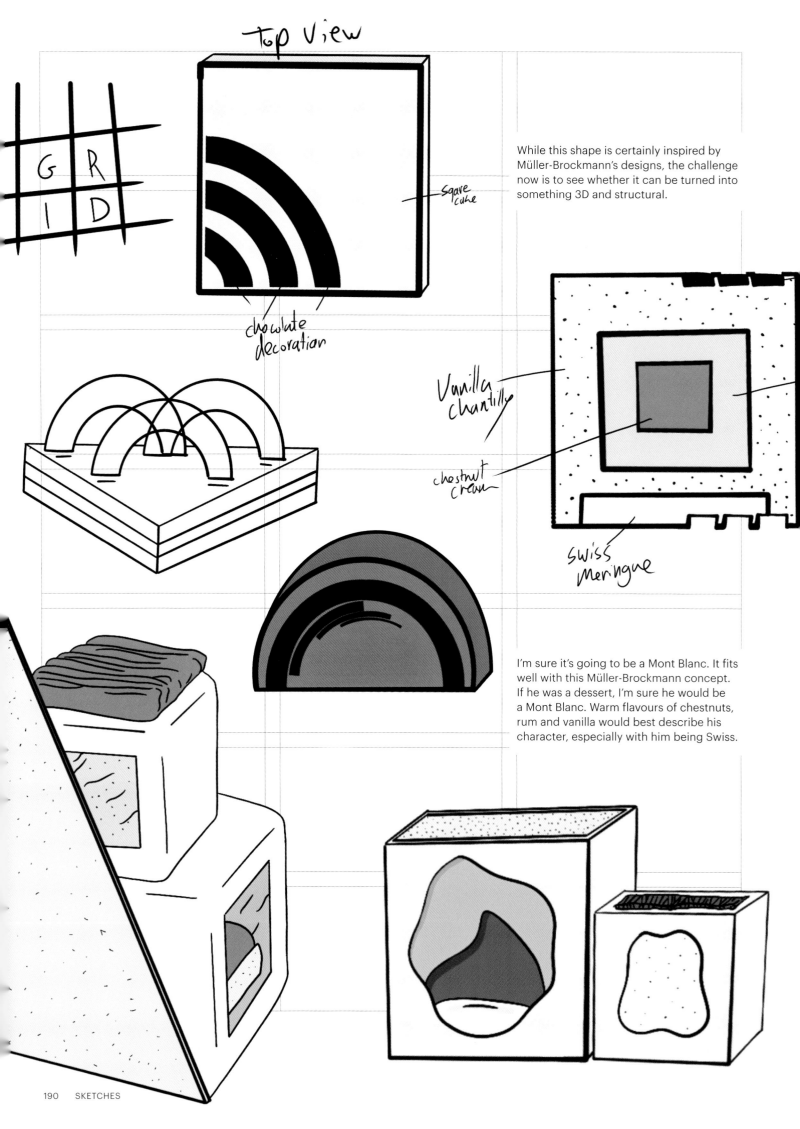

Top View

GRID

square cube

chocolate decoration

While this shape is certainly inspired by Müller-Brockmann's designs, the challenge now is to see whether it can be turned into something 3D and structural.

Vanilla chantilly

chestnut cream

Swiss Meringue

I'm sure it's going to be a Mont Blanc. It fits well with this Müller-Brockmann concept. If he was a dessert, I'm sure he would be a Mont Blanc. Warm flavours of chestnuts, rum and vanilla would best describe his character, especially with him being Swiss.

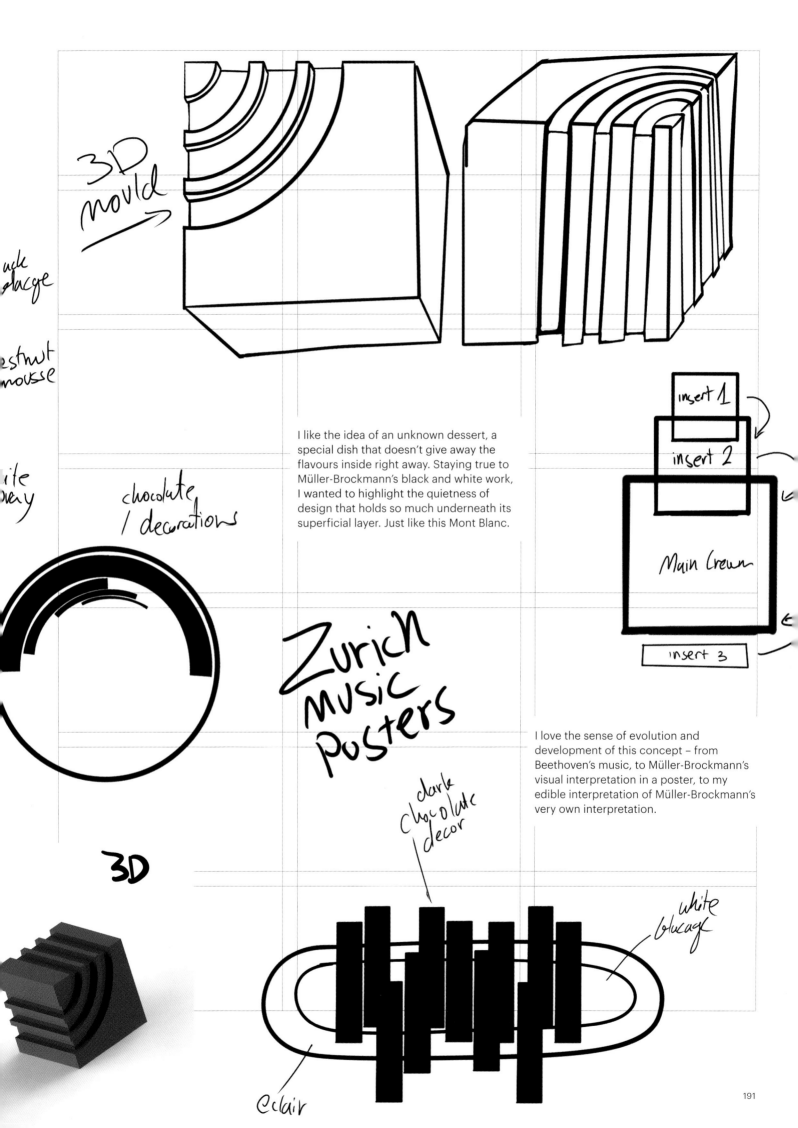

3D mould

chocolate / decorations

Zurich music posters

3D

dark chocolate decor

éclair

white blucage

insert 1

insert 2

Main Cream

insert 3

I like the idea of an unknown dessert, a special dish that doesn't give away the flavours inside right away. Staying true to Müller-Brockmann's black and white work, I wanted to highlight the quietness of design that holds so much underneath its superficial layer. Just like this Mont Blanc.

I love the sense of evolution and development of this concept – from Beethoven's music, to Müller-Brockmann's visual interpretation in a poster, to my edible interpretation of Müller-Brockmann's very own interpretation.

Chestnut cream insert

125 g   chestnut paste
125 g   chestnut cream
25 g   butter noisette
20 g   heavy cream
½   vanilla bean
10 g   rum

Make the butter noisette by cooking the butter on medium heat until the butter turns brown and has a nut like scent and let it cool. In a stand mixer with the paddle attachment, mix the chestnut cream and chestnut paste until fully combined. Next, slowly add the cooled butter noisette followed by the heavy cream, the vanilla and them rum until combine. Pass this through a sieve and pipe it into a square mould.

Chestnut mousse insert

113 g   milk
½   vanilla pod
20 g   sugar
32 g   yolks
17 g   gelatin mass
62 g   chestnut paste
62 g   chestnut cream
100 g   heavy cream

In a saucepan, add the vanilla pod to the milk and bring it to almost boil, and make a crème anglaise (see page 7) adding the sugar and yolks. Remove from the heat. Add the gelatin mass and mix well. Strain and pour over the chestnut cream and chestnut paste. Mix using a hand blender and let the preparation cool. Meanwhile, whip the heavy cream, fold it into the mix and pipe it into the square insert mould.

Swiss meringue

210 g   icing sugar
1   vanilla pod
105 g   egg whites
         Zéphyr™ 34% white chocolate
         (for brushing)

In a bain-marie, heat the egg whites, icing sugar and vanilla to 50°C while constantly stirring with a whisk (but not vigorously whisking!). Once at temperature, move to the stand mixer and mix using the whipping attachment, until hard peaks form.

Immediately spread the meringue on a silicone mat to a thickness of around 1 cm and, using a square cookie cutter dipped in oil, cut squares in the meringue. Bake at 80°C for 4–5 hours or until completely dry.

Let the meringue cool completely, then brush the white chocolate all around it Let it set until the chocolate firm.

Black glaçage

75 g   water
150 g   glucose
100 g   sugar
50 g   inverted sugar
100 g   condensed milk
70 g   gelatin mass
150 g   Mexique 66% dark chocolate
         black colouring

In a saucepan, bring the water, glucose, sugar and inverted sugar to a boil. Pour the preparation over the gelatin mass and the condensed milk and mix well with a hand blender. Next, add the chocolate, the black colouring and mix again.

Let it rest overnight in the fridge and use at 36–38°C.

Vanilla chantilly

150 g   heavy cream (1)
72 g   sugar
1   vanilla pod
63 g   gelatin mass
600 g   heavy cream (2)

In a pan, bring the heavy cream (1) sugar and vanilla pod to an almost boil. Remove from the heat and add the gelatin. Mix well with a hand blender. Add the heavy cream (2) and mix everything again. Cool the preparation overnight before whipping.

White spray

80 g   Zéphyr™ 34% white chocolate
100 g   cacao butter
         white colouring

Melt the white chocolate and cacao butter. Add the white colouring and mix well with a hand blender. Spray this mixture at around 34°C.

Decoration and construction

Take the frozen chestnut cream and place it inside the chestnus mousse. Let it freeze. Once harden, pipe the vanilla chantilly inside a square mould and place the insert of the chestnut mouse inside. Add the meringue on top. Freeze again.

When ready, remove from the mould, spray with the white spray and decorate with black glaçage.

XIII

CAMPARI & ORANGE

CAMPARI & ORANGE

I'm not your regular alcohol fan. I never have been. I drink occasionally, mostly when I'm out for dinner or just with friends, then I might have a glass of wine or a cocktail. But, if there is one drink that I do love, it's Campari & orange.

That wonderful bitterness and acidic sweetness, the summery feeling you get when you have a sip of its freshness – it's just the perfect combination for me. Having said that, I grew up with orange cake, a national weekend dessert at home (not only at my home, but all around the country) and I never really liked any version of it. It was always too dry (we call it "choke cake") and, to me, it never tasted like orange, due to unbalanced recipes that overshadowed the orange juice inside.

One of my goals here is to make a really good orange cake, with that orange zing in every bite. And to it, I want to add some Campari that will give the cake a little kick with extra bitterness. But definitely the star of this creation should be the cake... I want this dessert to look like a Campari orange cocktail – almost drinkable. So, as you can imagine, I've already started planning to make a special mould. I want to keep it simple. Not too many textures and flavours, just like the real drink. This will make the cake light and fun to eat, especially when it's hot outside and you're in need of a cold cocktail.

As I am going to make a special mould, I'm thinking of which direction to take: low ball or high ball? Maybe it should be a version of "gâteau de voyage" that you cut slices of... or maybe just a single cocktail. Either way, I'll try both directions. I also want to explore potential textures for the cocktail glasses to see which will work best for my idea of filling an indent on the top of the glass with Campari jelly, like a jelly shot: fresh and alcoholic to complete the whole cocktail experience.

The colours must be some kind of gradient between yellow-orange-pink-red. I'm thinking of spraying the cake to get that gradient. And all in the name of research, I'm going to have to create (and taste) some Campari-orange cocktails and compare my recipes to the source.

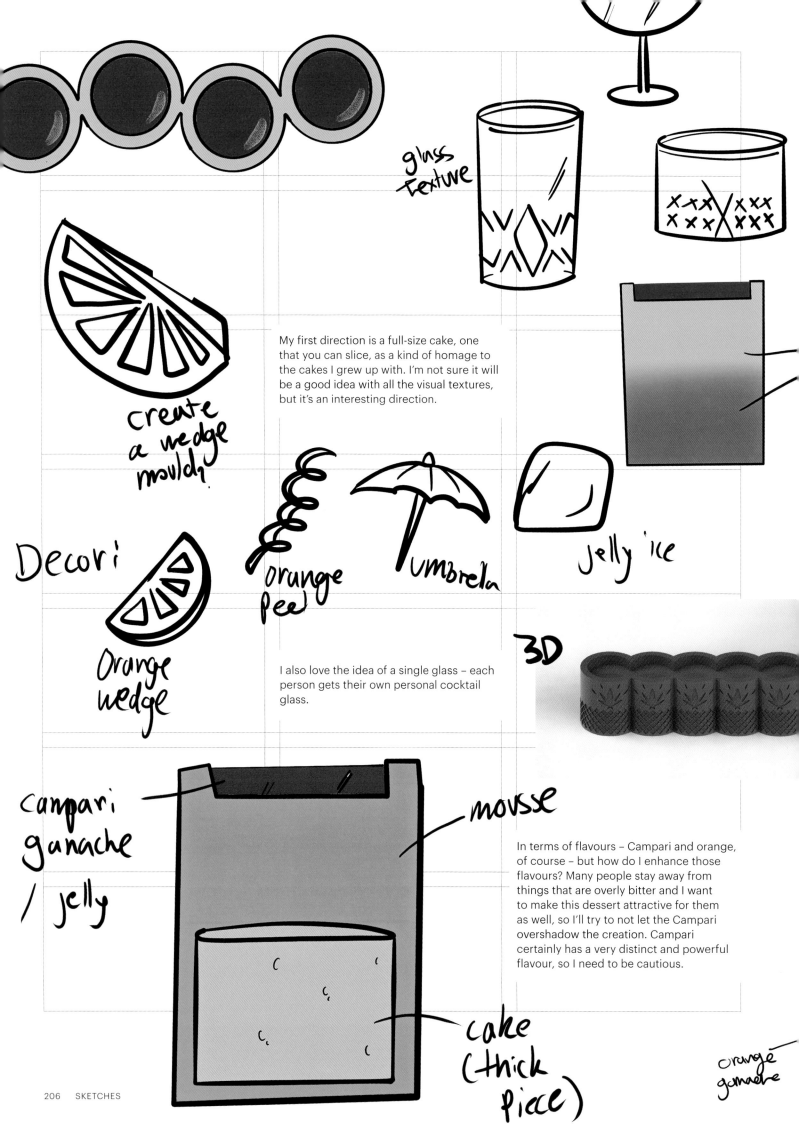

glass texture

create a wedge mould?

My first direction is a full-size cake, one that you can slice, as a kind of homage to the cakes I grew up with. I'm not sure it will be a good idea with all the visual textures, but it's an interesting direction.

Decori

orange peel

umbrella

Jelly ice

Orange wedge

I also love the idea of a single glass – each person gets their own personal cocktail glass.

3D

Campari ganache / Jelly

mousse

In terms of flavours – Campari and orange, of course – but how do I enhance those flavours? Many people stay away from things that are overly bitter and I want to make this dessert attractive for them as well, so I'll try to not let the Campari overshadow the creation. Campari certainly has a very distinct and powerful flavour, so I need to be cautious.

cake (thick piece)

orange ganache

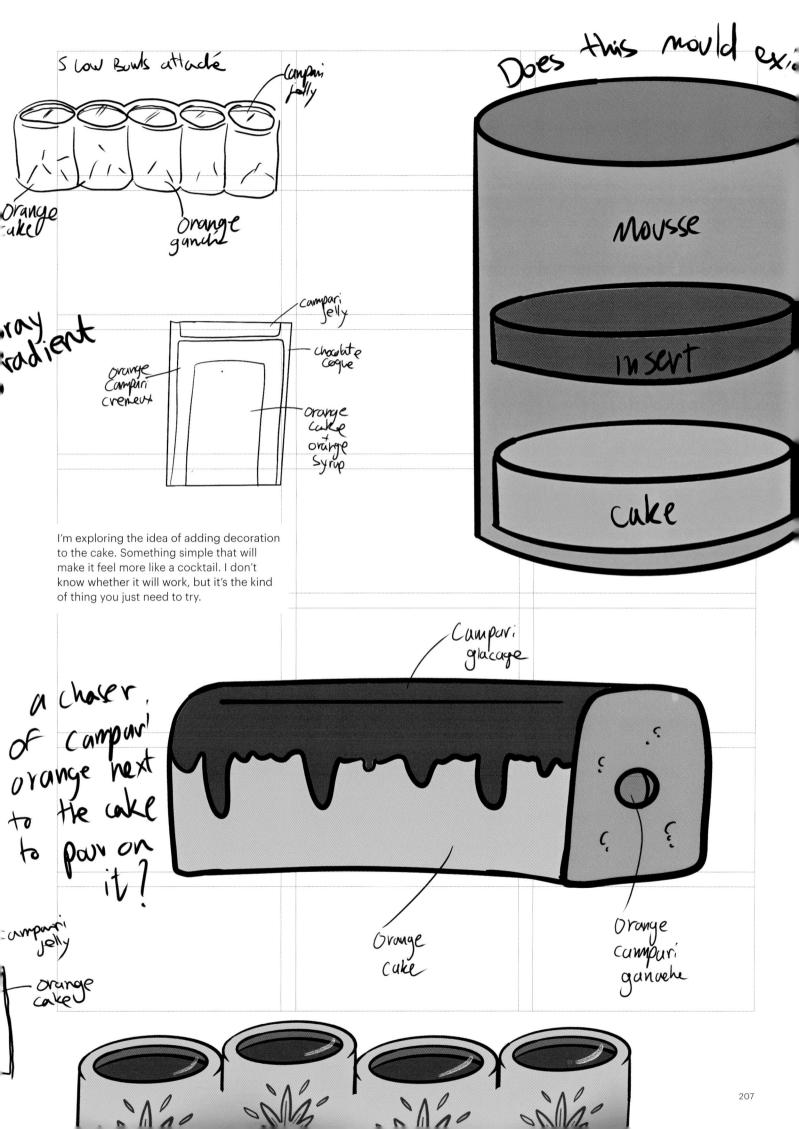

Slow Bowls attaché

Campari Jelly

Orange cake

Orange ganache

ray radient

Campari Jelly

chocolate coque

orange Campari cremeux

orange cake + orange syrup

I'm exploring the idea of adding decoration to the cake. Something simple that will make it feel more like a cocktail. I don't know whether it will work, but it's the kind of thing you just need to try.

Does this mould exi[...]

Mousse

insert

cake

Campari glaçage

a chaser of Campari orange next to the cake to pour on it?

Campari Jelly

orange cake

Orange cake

Orange Campari ganache

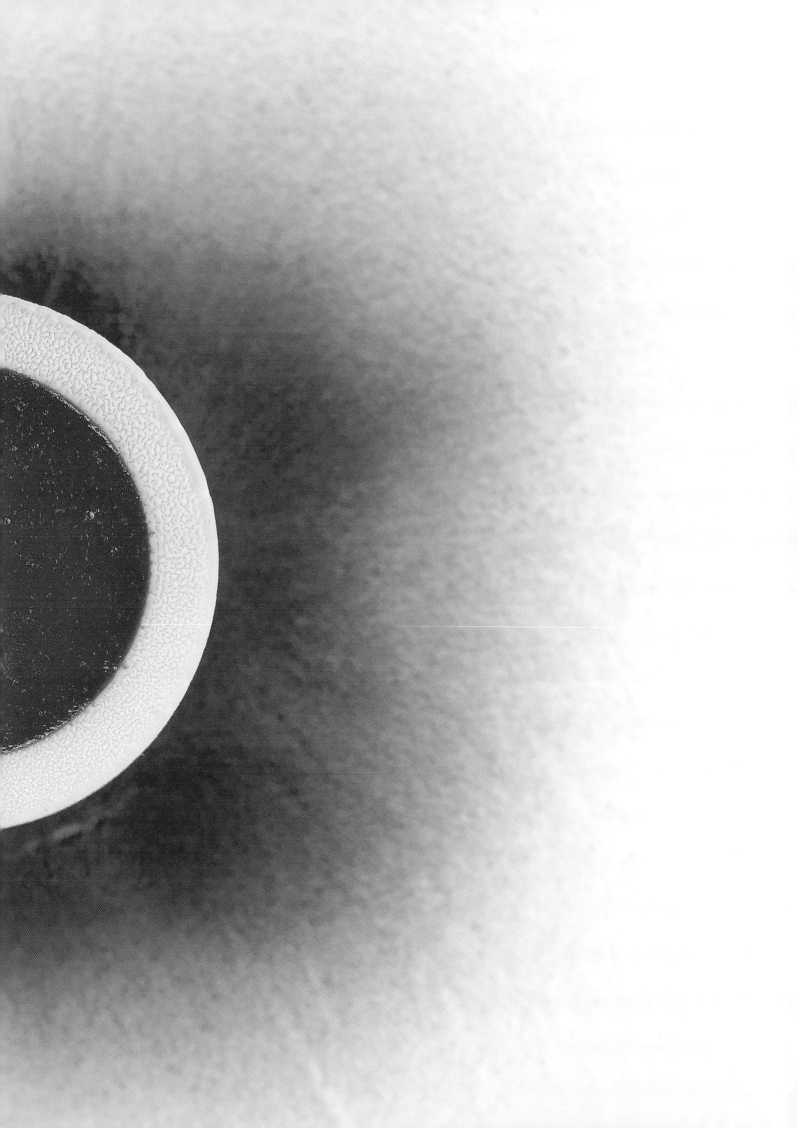

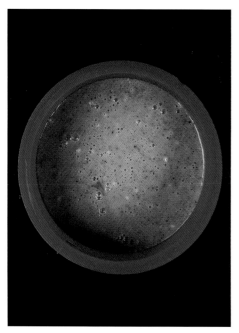

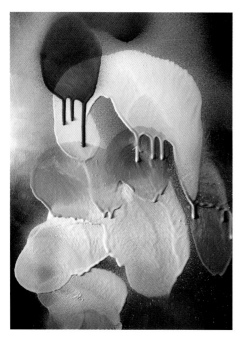

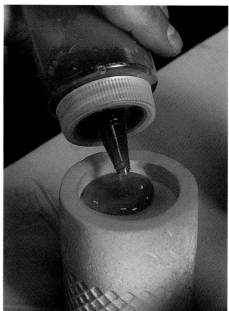

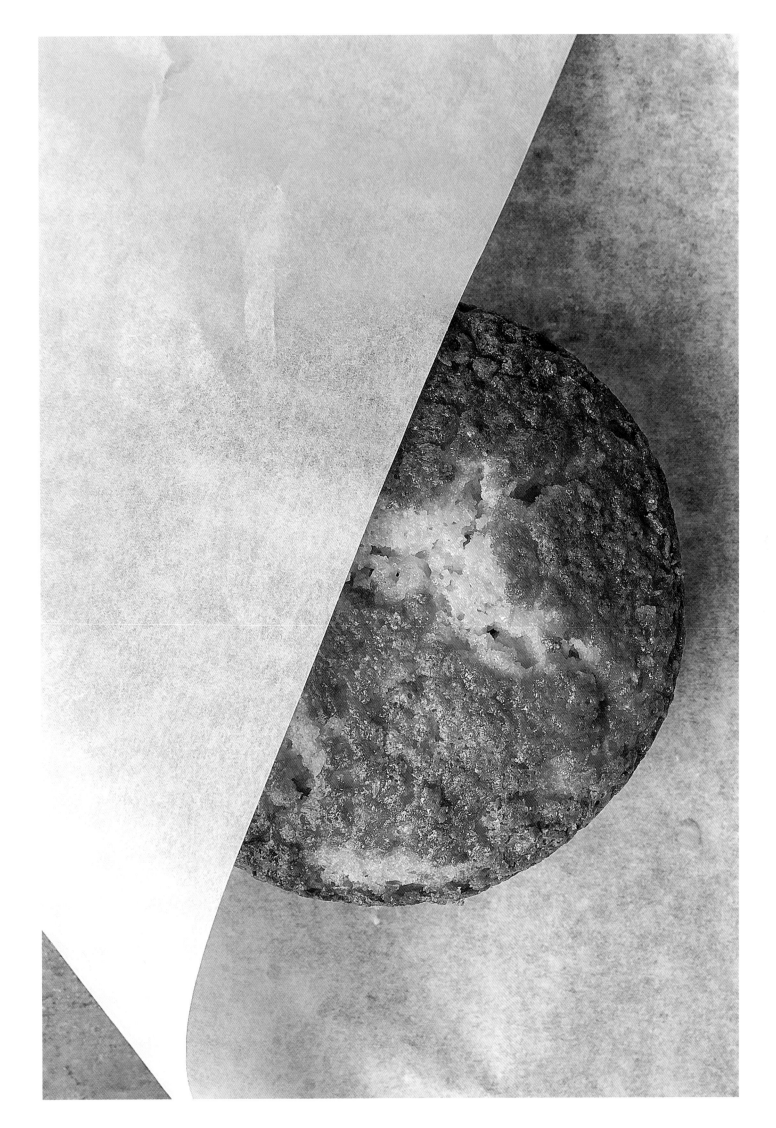

Orange cake

200 g   eggs
110 g   heavy cream
220 g   flour
12 g   baking powder
220 g   sugar
2 g   salt
115 g   olive oil
110 g   orange juice
30 g   orange zest
     orange juice for brushing

In a stand mixer with the paddle attachment, mix together the eggs and heavy cream. Add the sifted flour, baking powder, sugar and salt. Add the oil, orange zest and orange juice. Mix until well combined.

Bake in an 18 x 6 cm ring at 160°C for 1 hour and let it cool. Using a round cookie cutter, make the insert in the cake, and brush well with orange juice.

Campari™ orange chantilly

200 g   orange juice
315 g   heavy cream (1)
70 g   sugar
40 g   Campari™
10 g   zest
53 g   gelatin mass
150 g   mascarpone
325 g   heavy cream (2)

In a saucepan, reduce the orange juice from 200 g to 60 g.

Next add the cream (1), sugar, Campari and orange zest and bring it to a boil. Remove from heat.

Add the gelatin and mix. Then, add the mascarpone and mix well. Finally, add the cream (2) and mix before passing it through a sieve.

Let this mixture cool overnight before whipping.

Campari™ jelly

60 g   Campari™
20 g   water
1 g   agar agar
20 g   sugar
38 g   gelatin mass
20 g   lemon juice
     orange/red spray

In a saucepan, heat the Campari, the water, the agar agar and sugar to boil.

Remove from the heat and add the lemon juice followed by the gelatin mass. Let cool before use.

Orange/red spray

80 g   Zéphyr™ 34% white chocolate
100 g   cacao butter
     red/orange colouring

Melt the cacao butter and the white chocolate to 34°C. Add the orange colouring and mix with a hand blender before spraying with spray gun.

Repeat with the red colouring.

Decoration and construction

Make the orange cake, let it cool and cut circle inserts with a cookie cutter. Fill the moulds with the orange Campari chantilly and place the orange cake inserts inside the chantilly. Freeze completely.

Spray the top part with yellow colour and the bottom part with red colour. Pour the jelly on to the top part.

XIV

MIDNIGHT IN PARIS

It's been eight years since I moved to Paris to fulfil my pastry dreams and there is nothing more inspiring than the beauty of this city. When I first moved here, it was a lot to take in – every street you walk down has its charm and every hour of the day has its own magic, it all feels like a scene from a movie. You go out at night to buy something and you see the Eiffel Tower sparkling... If you look out of the window at a certain time of night a huge light beam will find you from the depths of the 16th arrondissement. Even after eight years of living here, I am still captivated by where I live.

It always reminds me of the Woody Allen movie, *Midnight in Paris* in which the city's historical characters come out to party at night, and how a scene from 80 years ago can look similar to today. That is why I also have huge respect for the conservation of this city and its stunning facade.

This creation is a token of my love for this city. I want to capture how I feel when I lookout of the window or walk down the street. Just try crossing a bridge over the Seine at night and you will understand exactly what I mean.

Paris at night is my main inspiration and a big part of my mood board, but also the moon, looking over the city center, surrounded by these dark buildings and small night lights. I want to capture a moment here that will convey a feeling every person who has visited or lived in Paris will relate to. The danger of using Paris in art is that you can quickly head into cliché territories, but there's no way around it – Paris is a bit of a cliché, and I mean that in the best way possible. Every image of this place is associated with romance, love, history, art, food, and even particular scents. It is the beauty and the curse of being such an iconic place, and I want to have my own version of it. Because we all have our own vision of what Paris is like.

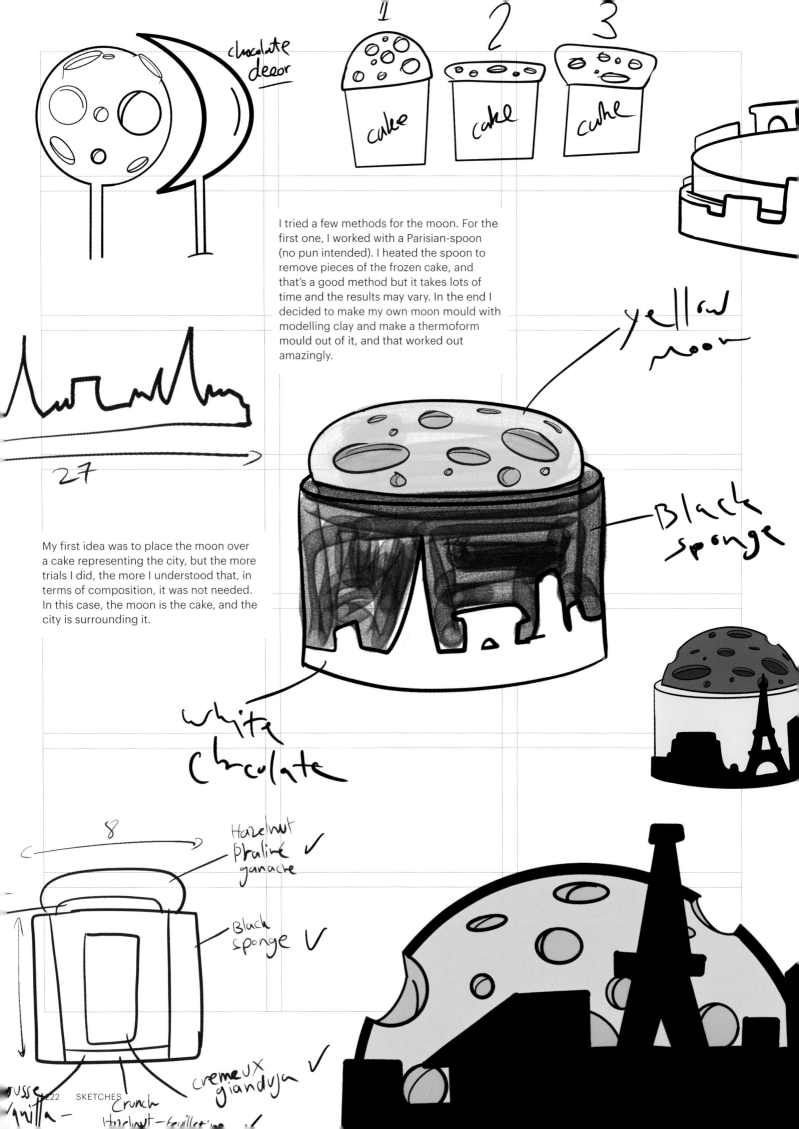

chocolate decor

1

2

3

cake

cake

cube

I tried a few methods for the moon. For the first one, I worked with a Parisian-spoon (no pun intended). I heated the spoon to remove pieces of the frozen cake, and that's a good method but it takes lots of time and the results may vary. In the end I decided to make my own moon mould with modelling clay and make a thermoform mould out of it, and that worked out amazingly.

yellow moon

27

My first idea was to place the moon over a cake representing the city, but the more trials I did, the more I understood that, in terms of composition, it was not needed. In this case, the moon is the cake, and the city is surrounding it.

Black sponge

white Chocolate

8

Hazelnut Praliné ganache ✓

Black sponge ✓

cremeux gianduja ✓

Mousse vanilla —

Crunch Hazelnut—Feuilletine

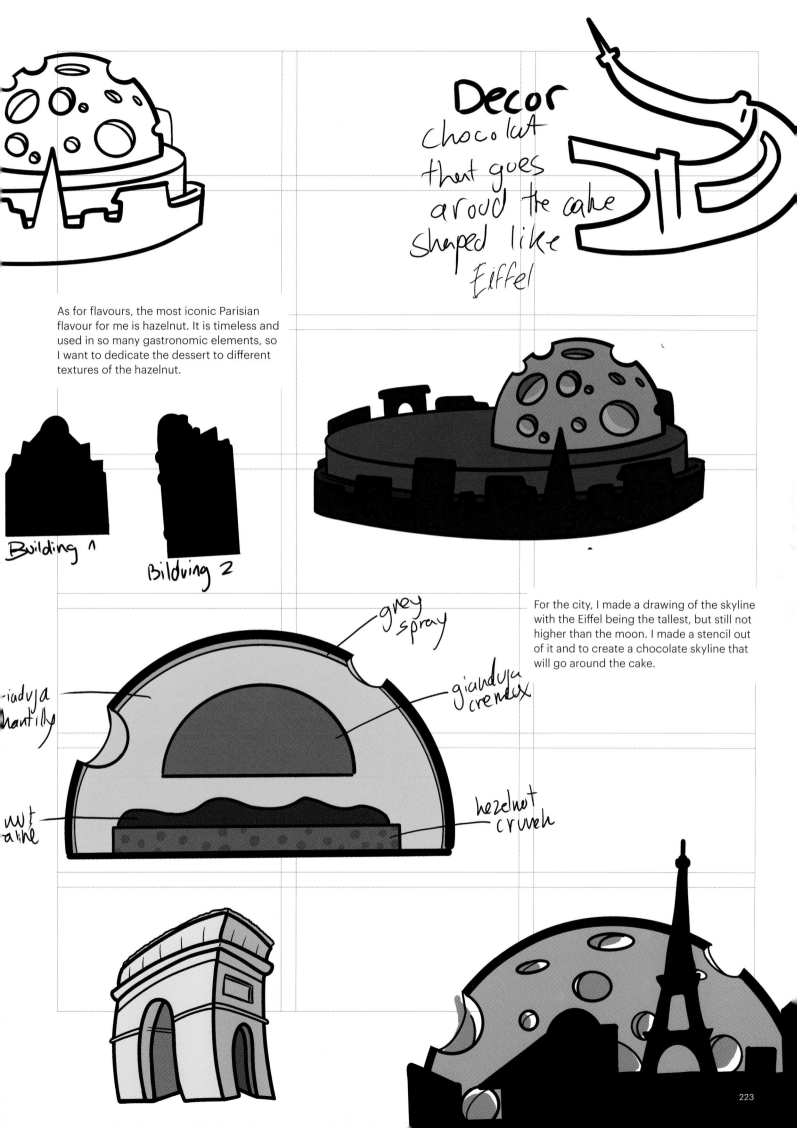

Decor
chocolat
that goes
aroud the cake
shaped like
Eiffel

As for flavours, the most iconic Parisian flavour for me is hazelnut. It is timeless and used in so many gastronomic elements, so I want to dedicate the dessert to different textures of the hazelnut.

Building 1

Bildving 2

grey spray

gianduja crendex

-iaduja hantilly

nut aline

hezelnot cruveh

For the city, I made a drawing of the skyline with the Eiffel being the tallest, but still not higher than the moon. I made a stencil out of it and to create a chocolate skyline that will go around the cake.

223

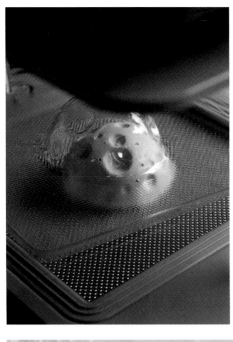

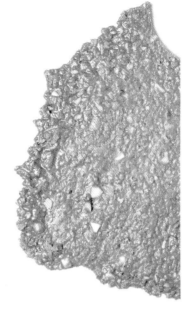

Gianduja crémeux

52 g	yolks
215 g	heavy cream
32 g	gelatin mass
205 g	milk chocolate gianduja
80 g	Inaya™ 65% dark chocolate

In a saucepan, bring the heavy cream and yolks to 82°C while constantly stirring. Remove from the heat, add the gelatin mass and mix together.

Through a sieve pour the mix over the chopped gianduja and dark chocolate, and mix with a hand blender. Finally, pour the preparation into the demi-sphère insert mould and freeze.

Hazelnut praliné

225 g	hazelnuts
160 g	sugar
40 g	water
1/2	vanilla pod
2 g	salt

Toast the hazelnuts until light brown and remove the shells if needed.

In a saucepan, heat the sugar and water to 118°C.

Once at temperature, add the hazelnuts and mix well until caramelised.

Pour over a silicone mat and let the caramelised nuts cool completely.

Next, in a food processor, place the caramelised nuts with the salt and vanilla and grind until it reaches a semi-liquid texture. Finally, pipe the preparation in small discs moulds the same size as the crémeux inserts, and freeze.

Hazelnut crunch

75 g	Alunga™ 41% milk chocolate
120 g	pure hazelnut paste
3 g	salt
30 g	chopped hazelnuts
60 g	feuilletine

Melt the milk chocolate and mix it with all the remaining ingredients.

Freeze and then cut with a round cookie cutter that has smaller diameter than the mould.

Grey spray

80 g	Zéphyr™ 34% white chocolate
100 g	cacao butter
	black colouring

Melt the cacao butter and the white chocolate to 34°C. Add the black colouring and mix with a hand blender before spraying with spray gun.

Gianduja chantilly

75 g	heavy cream (1)
120 g	milk chocolate gianduja
18 g	gelatin mass
225 g	heavy cream (2)

Heat the heavy cream (1) until it almost reaches a boil. Remove from heat and add the gelatin mass. Soften the gianduja in a microwave and pour the heavy cream preparation on top of it. Mix everything together. Finally, add the heavy cream (2) and mix well with a hand blender.

Cool the mixture overnight before whipping.

Decoration and construction

Inaya™ 65% dark chocolate
black colouring

Fill the moon shaped demi-sphere mould with the gianduja chantilly.

Place the crémeux and praliné insert inside the chantilly. Cover with more chantilly and top with the hazelnut crunch. Freeze.

Once frozen, remove from the mould. Spray with the grey spray.

Finally, decorate the cake with the chocolate decoration.

To do so, make a stencil of the Paris skyline using cutting printer (see page 7), long enough to go around the cake. Cover the stencil with a thin layer of black tempered chocolate and place it around a ring the same diameter as the cake. Let the chocolate set and remove the stencil slowly. Finaly, place the chocolate decoration around the cake.

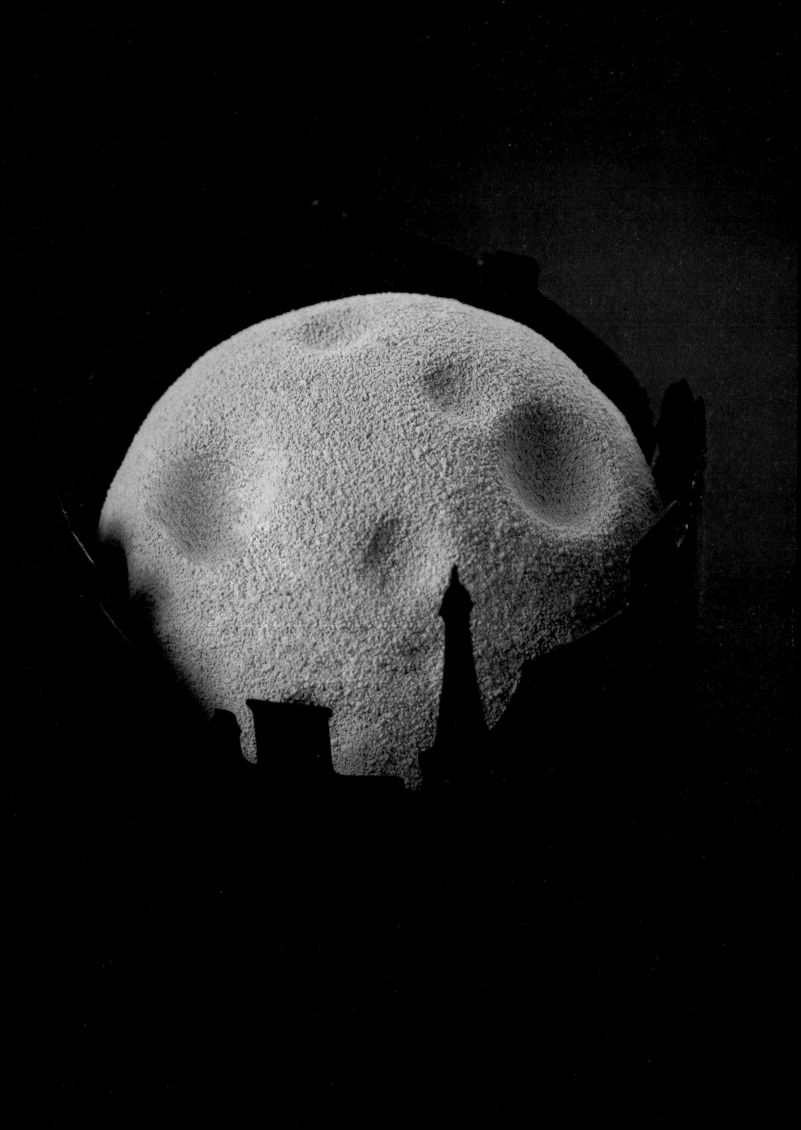

GALAXY

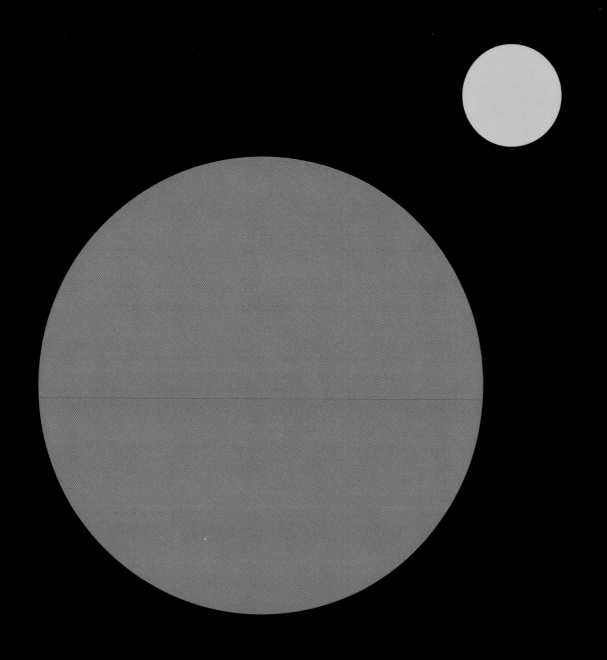

On December 21st, 2021, in an event that happens once every 20 years, for one night only, we got to witness the Jupiter and Saturn conjunction, which was extremely visible in the night sky. I came across the announcement of this rare event – also known as 'double planets' – by chance. Unfortunately, I didn't own a telescope at the time, but made sure to watch it on the internet the following day.

I've always been fascinated by outer space and worlds that are beyond our reach. I feel like when I understand how small we are compared to the infinity of space; it keeps me grounded. There is so much we don't know and can't see that exists outside of our general comprehension. If I hadn't turned into a pastry chef, I would have wanted to become an astronomer or, better yet, an astronaut!

This astronomical event resparked my interest in our solar system. Every time I look through that telescope, I feel like I am traveling to another universe. And there's always a moment in which my mind tells me it must be celebrated with my creativity. I want to create a dessert that looks like someone took a bite from outer space.

This creation will rely heavily on technique, but it will celebrate space in the most captivating way.

I want hints of stars, meteors, the milky way, and anything I can put into to my creation of a space constellation.

We all have our own image of what space looks like and for me it's a lot of blue, purple and green.

For my mood board, I knew would need to find a representation of Saturn and Jupiter, the Milky Way and of course the stars.

If I want to create a piece of the galaxy on to a cake, it should include the atmosphere of space too. The question is, how do I do this? Should I make a planet cake or present the entire solar system somehow? What I do know is, I want it to feature Jupiter...

It will be black in colour and offer a dramatic contrast against the brighter colours – red, yellow, blue etc.

Feb 28, 2021, 10:00pm EST

A Spectacular View Of Mars And A Jupiter-Mercury Fist-Bump: What You Can See In The Night Sky This Week

Saturn-Jupiter conjunction
Best time to view: from 4.30pm GMT December 21

Saturn
Jupiter
Sun
Earth

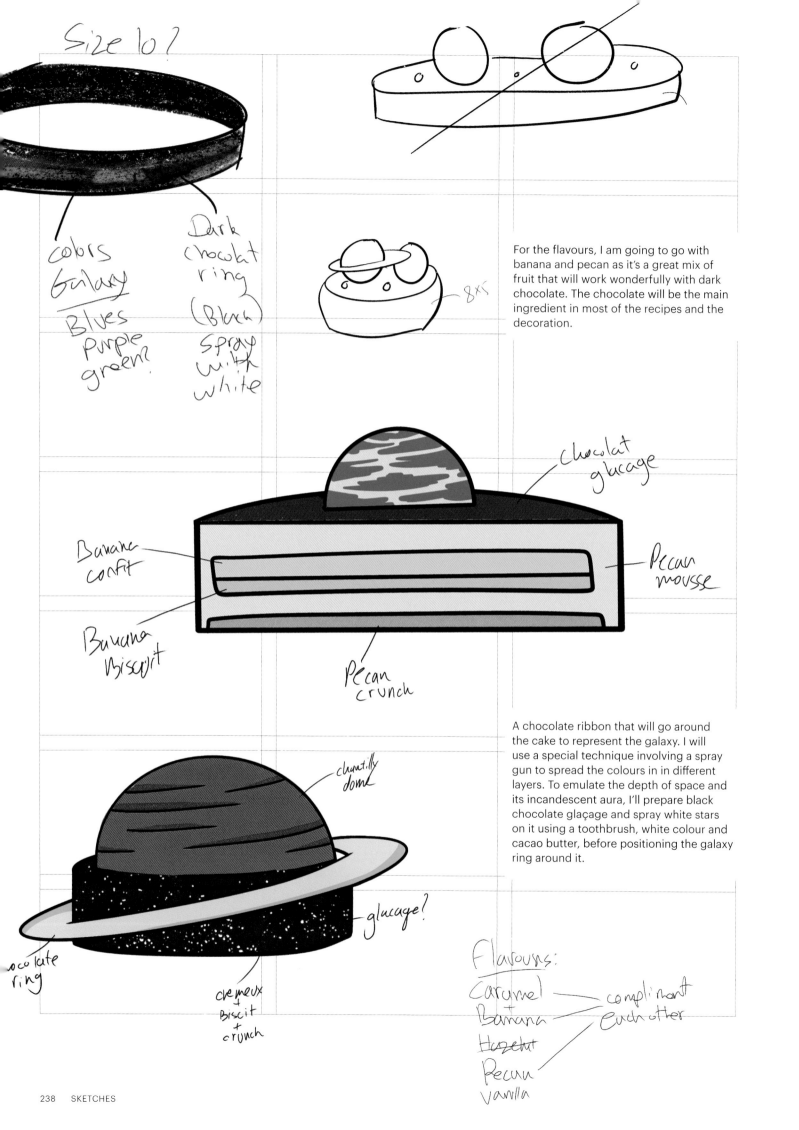

Size 10?

colors
Galaxy
Blues
Purple
green?

Dark
chocolat
ring
(Black)
Spray
with
white

8×5

For the flavours, I am going to go with banana and pecan as it's a great mix of fruit that will work wonderfully with dark chocolate. The chocolate will be the main ingredient in most of the recipes and the decoration.

Chocolat glacage

Banana confit

Pecan mousse

Banana biscuit

Pecan crunch

A chocolate ribbon that will go around the cake to represent the galaxy. I will use a special technique involving a spray gun to spread the colours in in different layers. To emulate the depth of space and its incandescent aura, I'll prepare black chocolate glaçage and spray white stars on it using a toothbrush, white colour and cacao butter, before positioning the galaxy ring around it.

chantilly dome

glacage?

chocolate ring

cremeux + biscit + crunch

Flavours:
Caramel
+
Banana
Hazelnut
Pecan
vanilla

compliment
each other

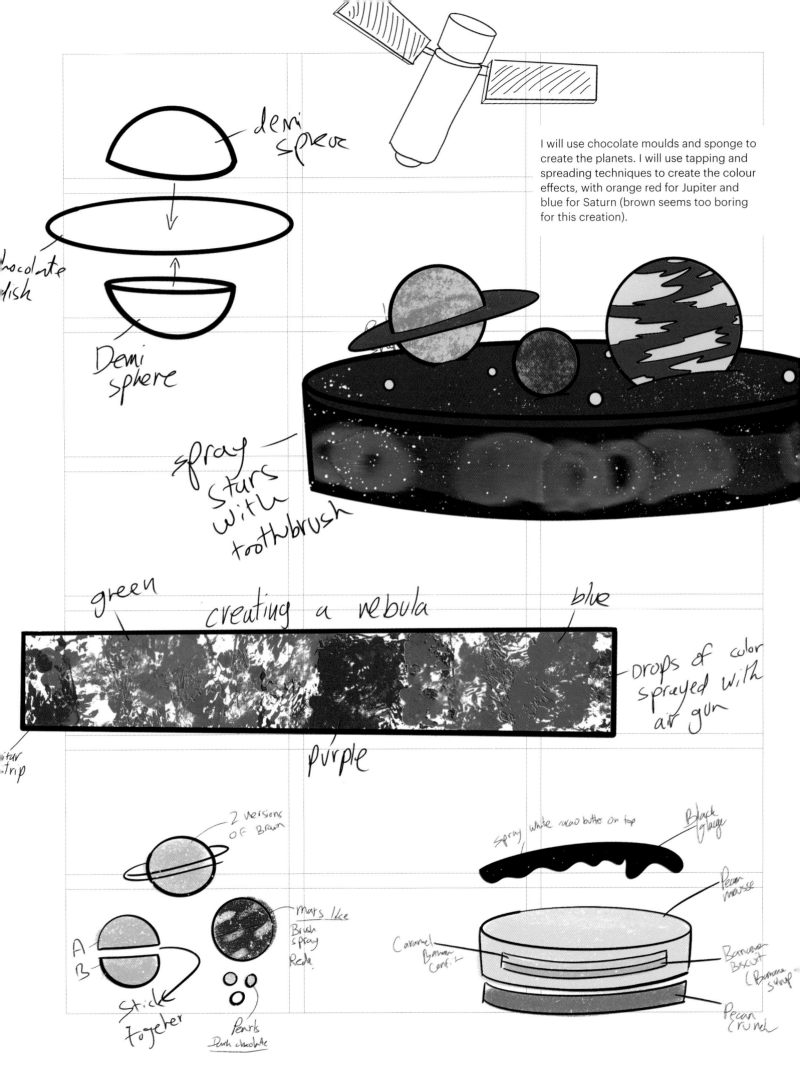

demi spere

chocolate dish

Demi sphere

I will use chocolate moulds and sponge to create the planets. I will use tapping and spreading techniques to create the colour effects, with orange red for Jupiter and blue for Saturn (brown seems too boring for this creation).

spray Stars with toothbrush

green

creating a nebula

blue

purple

drops of color sprayed with air gun

star strip

2 versions of Brown

Mars like Brush spray Reds.

A
B

Stick Together

Pearls
Dark chocolate

Spray white cacao butter on top

Black Glaze

Pecan Mousse

Caramel Banana Conf.

Banana Biscuit (Banana Syrup)

Pecan Crunch

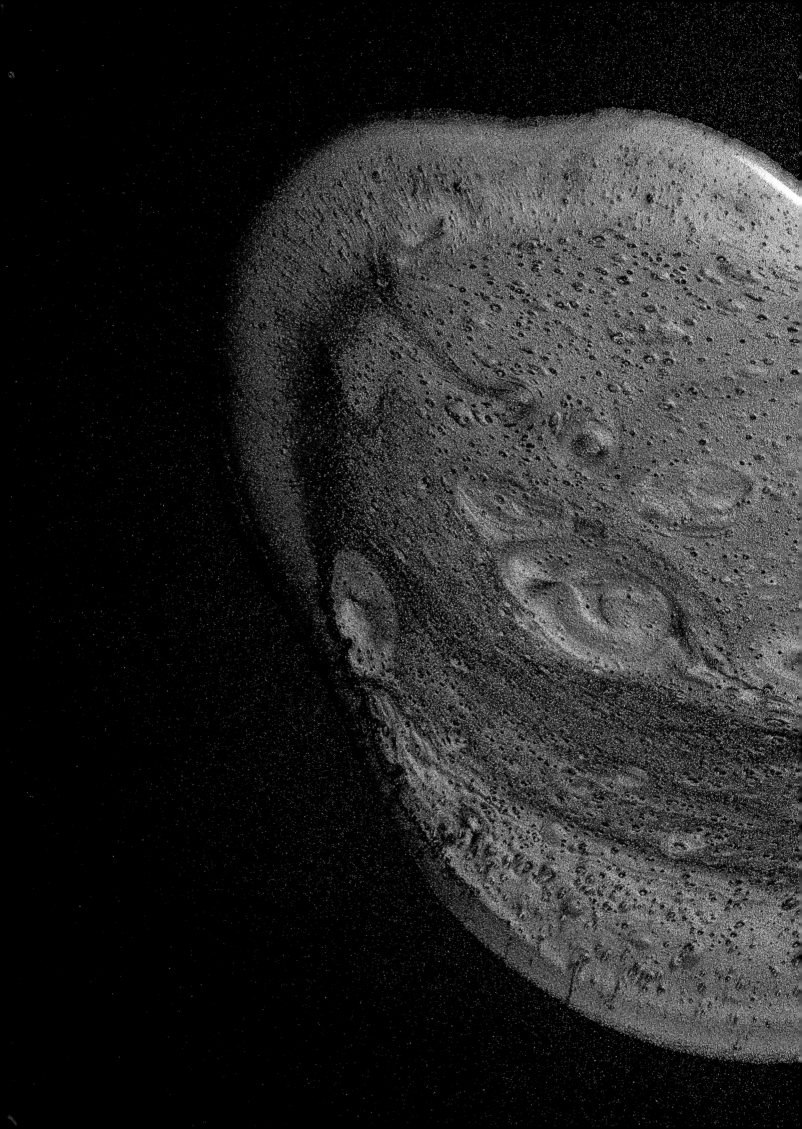

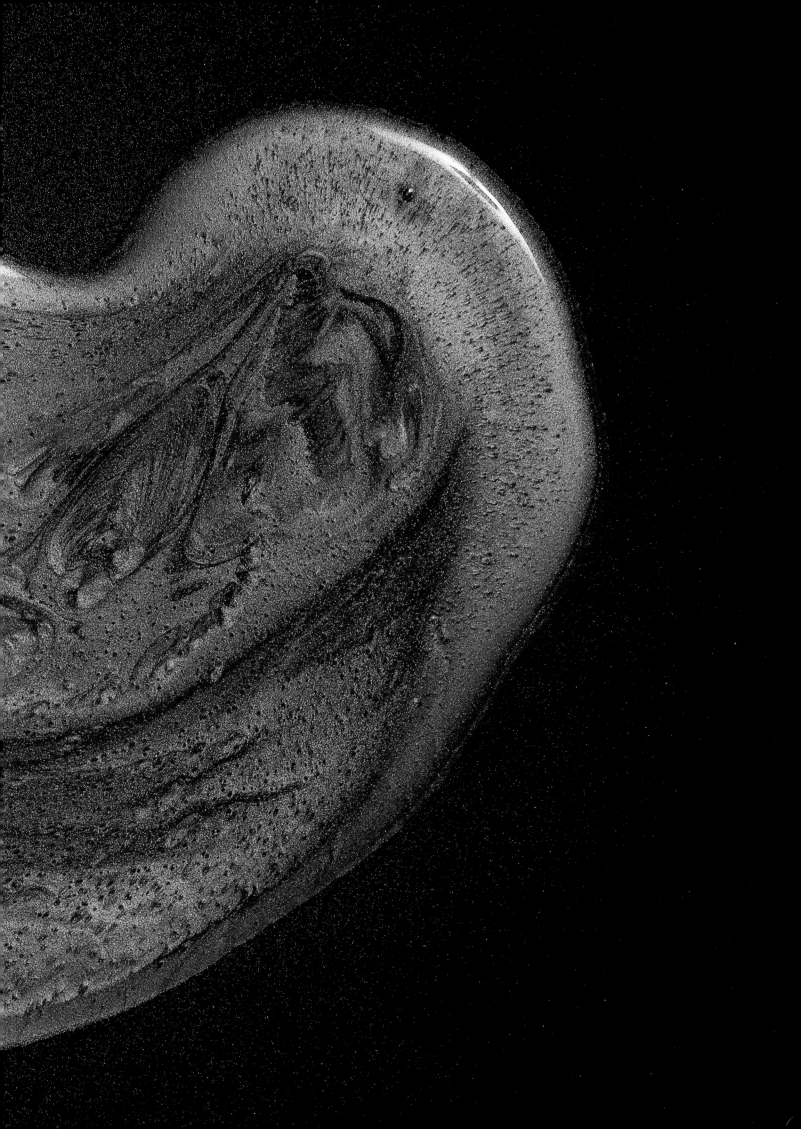

Pecan mousse

100 g	milk
150 g	heavy cream (1)
40 g	sugar
50 g	yolks
200 g	Zéphyr™ 34% white chocolate
28 g	gelatin mass
100 g	pure pecan paste
400 g	heavy cream (2)

In a saucepan, heat the milk and cream (1) and bring to almost boil.

Separately, mix the yolks and the sugar and make a crème anglaise (see page 7), and bring to boil.

Remove from the heat, add the gelatin mass and mix well. Using a sieve, pour the preparation over the white chocolate and pecan paste and mix with a hand blender. Let it cool completely.

Finally, whip the cream (2) and fold it into the mixture.

Banana confit

30 g	glucose
80 g	sugar
150 g	heavy cream
½	vanilla pod
450 g	banana puree
30 g	lemon juice
66 g	gelatin mass

Make a caramel by adding sugar to the glucose, little by little, until caramel forms.

Separately, heat the heavy cream to a boil and slowly add in the caramel. Mix until well combined over low heat.

Next, add the banana puree and vanilla to the preparation and bring it to a boil.

Banana biscuit

380 g	marzipan
265 g	eggs
130 g	fresh bananas
125 g	olive oil
120 g	flour
38 g	potato starch
4 g	salt
165 g	egg whites
50 g	sugar

In a stand mixer, using the paddle attachment, mix the marzipan and the eggs together

Next, change to the whipping attachment and add the banana and the oil. Sift in the flour and then potato starch. Finally add some salt and whip until light and airy.

Separately, whip the egg whites and the sugar and fold it into the marzipan preparation. Spread on a silicone matt to reach a 0.8 thickness, and bake at 190°C for around 8 minutes.

Lastly, soak the warm biscuit with the banana syrup.

Pecan crunch

45 g	Zéphyr™ 34% white chocolate
15 g	cacao butter
160 g	pure pecan paste
2 g	salt
50 g	feuilletine
60 g	pecan
30 g	dried banana
47 g	granola

Melt the chocolate and cacao butter together and add the pecan paste. Mix in all the dry ingredients. Roll onto a silicone mat to create a thin layer and place in the fridge. Once harden, cut some circles using a cookie cutter smaller than the cake

Chocolate glaçage

75 g	water
150 g	glucose
100 g	sugar
50 g	inverted sugar
70 g	gelatin mass
100 g	condensed milk
150 g	Mexique 66% dark chocolate
	black colouring

In a saucepan, heat the water, glucose, inverted sugar and sugar and bring to a boil. Pour over the gelatin mass and condensed milk and combine well. Add the chocolate and black colouring and mix again.

Let this rest overnight and reheat before use at 36–38°C.

Colour for chocolate

100 g	cacao butter
5 g	black colouring

Melt the cacao butter, add the colouring and mix well with a hand blender. Then temper to 27°C before use.

Repeat this process for red, white, purple and blue colouring.

Banana syrup

150 g	water
130 g	sugar
100 g	banana puree

Heat the water and the sugar and bring to a boil. Remove from the heat and add the banana puree. Mix well.

Decoration and construction

Mexique 66% dark chocolate
black colouring

Place in an insert the banana biscuit
brushed with the banana syrup. Top it with
the banana confit and freeze.

Pipe the pecan mousse into a larger mould
or ring and place the frozen banana biscuit
insert.

Place the pecan crunch on top and freeze.

Once frozen, remove from the freezer and
pour the black glaçage over the frozen
cake.

Using a brush and a knife, spread the white
colouring to create a 'star' effect.

Place acetate stripes the same height as
the cake on a flat surface.

Using a brush and a knife, spread the white
colouring over the acetate stripes to create
a 'star' effect and let set.

Add drops of the blue and purple tempered
colouring in random places and, and using
only the air of a spray gun, spread the
colours carefully. Let it set and then spread
a thin layer of tempered black chocolate.
When the chocolate starts to set, place
each stripe around a ring the same size as
the cake and let it set .

Inside a demi-sphere chocolate mould, use
different techniques such as brush strokes
or use a sponge to tap different textures
inside the mould using the tempered
colouring (see making off spread of the
chapter). Let set.

Then cover with tempered black chocolate
and remove excess so that the demi-
sphere is hollow. Let see completely before
placing over the finished cake.

Merci de Tal

First and foremost, I would like to thank my partner for this project – Nathanaël Djimblith, a truly talented photographer who has been on board since the moment we sat in a Parisian cafe together and I told him about this crazy project. Thank you, Nate, for believing in this book and in the process, for being such a professional and, most importantly, a great friend for life. And even more than that, thanks for catching me when I was about to fall off that ladder!

I want to thank Cacao Barry for believing in this project from the get-go. Thank you, Andrea, for understanding my vision and trusting me and Nate, and most of all for allowing us to work with two incredible chefs: Ramon Morato, my personal role model who embodies what a chef should be like – modest, happy and super talented. Thank you, Ramon, for forming an important part of this book and for helping me elevate each dessert to the max. And you, Xavi, thank you for all the help and patience during this process.
You are as remarkable a person as you are a chef.

Special thanks to Florian from *Pastry Evo* for all the help with creating some crazy moulds.

I want to thank my talented friend, Ron, for his 3D skills and Tephanie for her pastry skills and our shared love for fries.

Thank you Adar, Dafna and Yonatan, for being there for me around the clock, whenever I needed consulting on anything to do with the book.

Thank you, Pepe, for supporting me throughout this whole time, when I was most stressed and anxious about getting this book just right. I love you.

Thank you mom for passing on to me your love for baking and making other people happy. And to my big brother, Mor, thank you for the support and wise advices, even though I'm taller than you.

Thanks, Zvika, for your help with the Bauhaus research and being such a supportive friend and photographer. And a big thank you to the people I love for all the advice along the way: Inbal, Tamar, Ari, Guri, Tuta, Ju, Benz, Mudi, Rona, Oren, Bjorn, Jerome & Nico, Barry, Dan, Manoela, Shine, Nicolas Guercio, Flore and so on...

Last but not least, I want to thank Francois, the editor of this book. Although we quickly discovered we are complete opposites, he believed in the concept and went along with my crazy ideas – but he also knew when to veto them. He made this book what it is through hard work and long hours along with Daniel, the designer who did a great job on this beautiful end result.

And if you have read this far, thank you for your interest and curiosity in my work.

I would like to finish with a quote that has been following me for years now:

"I once broke up with someone for not offering me pie."
– Elaine Benes

Tal Spiegel

249

Thank you from Nathanaël

Following years of international business studies and an initial career in procurement, it became obvious that I couldn't run from my destiny and embrace what has been a passion for years, photography.

There is an African proverb I can really relate to, that says: "It takes a village to raise a child". Indeed, there are countless people I could thank for helping me become the man and the photographer I am today.

First off, I want to thank Manoela Petrykowska, my sister from another mother. She pushed me into the water, so to speak, to become a professional photographer in my early 30s. I have had unbelievable experiences as a photographer, ones I couldn't have ever imagined. Some of them being with Cacao Barry. Thanks to Cacao Barry and Manoela, I ended up meeting Tal who became a dear friend through time.

Thank you, Tal for including me in this project – one I view as a true collaboration between two friends. Thank you for trusting me from the start. You gave me the space to share my ideas and allowed me to express myself as a photographer. You gave a me an insidelook at the work of a pastry chef. I believe this project has already made me a much better photographer and "business man". Dealing with the loss of my father earlier this year, this book has been one of the few things that kept me going and helped me move on with life.

What a journey this book has been... all these trips, these flavours and the people we met, including François and NHP...

I can never thank you enough.

I also want to thank Geraldine Martens, another great photographer and great friend of mine who really followed all the steps from the genesis to the print of this book. Thank you for all of your advice and for helping me deal with all the stress related to the making of the book.

Thank you to all my friends I did not mention by name, my brothers, my sister, my mother and my father, who have always supported me.

And last but not least, thank you to my sweeties, Hakeem and Sarah, my anchors, the 2/3s of me – I wouldn't be here if it wasn't for you. You two impact my life the most and in so many ways. You are probably the only ones who have to deal with "the real me" on a daily basis – my flaws, my emotions, the late nights, my travel for work. Thank you for being there, for sharing both my successes and my failures, and supporting me. I love you guys.

Nathanaël Djimbilth, French-Congolese photographer based between Paris and Fribourg (Switzerland).

250

Credits

Apple Twist (*mood board spread*)
Photos by Adam Nir, Marek Studzinski, Simon Lee, Rumana S, Marina Prodanović, Tomasz Filipek, Zoe Schaeffer, Yaya The Creator, Brian Patrick Tagalog & Ghislaine Guerin on Unsplash
Photo by Nathanaël Djimbilth

Bauhaus (*mood board spread*)
All photos by Tal Spiegel

Flamingo (*mood board spread*)
Photos by Edrick Krozendijk, Vicko Mozara, Etienne Girardet, Leandra Rieger, Marko Blažević, Henning Stein, Carlota Vidal, Jonathan Taylor, James Lee & Arno Senoner on Unsplash
Drawing by John Tenniel
Frame from Alice in Wonderland movie (1951) by Walt Disney pictures

Flower (*mood board spread*)
Photos by Prchi Palwe, Evie S, Allec Gomes, Janine Joles, Tiffany Nguyen, Annie Spratt & Shine Photos on Unsplash
Photo by Nathanaël Djimbilth
Photo by Iris Spiegel

Coral Reef (*mood board spread*)
Photos by Karo K, Francesco Ungaro (2 photos), Olena Shmahalo, David Clode, Ashley Byrd, Alexander Van Steenberge, Petr Sidorov, Birmingham Museums Trust, Shaun Low & Diane Picchiottino on Unsplash
Anna Pavlova in the Fokine/Saint-Saëns *The Dying Swan*, Saint Petersburg, 1905 – Unknown author

Lemon Squeezer (*mood board spread*)
All photos by Nathanaël Djimbilth

Volcano (*mood board spread*)
Photos by Ása Steinarsdóttir, Jonatan Pie, Martin Sanchez, Rishabh Pammi, Alex Sherstnev, Raphael Renter, Eugene Golovesov, Hunter So, Yousef Salhamoud & Bangsal Nam on Unsplash
Photo by Nathanaël Djimbilth

Fortune Teller (*mood board spread*)
Photos by Renè Müller, Michael Dziedzic, Petr Sidorov, Hulki Okan Tabak, Monique Pongan, Erol Ahmed & Mousum De on Unsplash
Photo by Matthew Kang
Illustration by Tal Spiegel
Photo by Nathanaël Djimbilth

Circus (*mood board spread*)
Photos by Laura Louise Grimsley, Jeremy Bezanger, Giorgio Trovato, Gabor Barbely, Albert Sukhanov, Jacqueline Brandwayn, Vitya Lapatey, Tom Hermans & Kentaro Toma on Unsplash
Photo by Nathanaël Djimbilth

Alien Abduction (*mood board spread*)
Photo by Albert Antony, Gianluca Carenza, Dmitrii Ko & Paul Green on Unsplash
Photo by Paul Trent in McMinnville, Oregon, USA 1950.
Photo from Department of Defense/AP
Photo from video of Lynne D. Kitei
Photo by Nathanaël Djimbilth
Photo by Tal Spiegel
Poster "I want to believe", X-Files series
Photo by Movie Poster Image Art/Getty Images
Logo from Mars Attacks movie

Malabi (*mood board spread*)
Photos by Kateryna Ivanova, Ameen Fahmy & Peter Fogden on Unsplash
Photos by Tal Spiegel

Müller-Brockmann (*mood board spread*)
All posters are by Josef Müller-Brockmann
Photo by Lars Müller Publishers

Campari & Orange (*mood board spread*)
Photos by Annie Spratt, Abhishek Hajare (2 photos), Dstudio Bcn, Riccardo Andolfo, Andrea Riezzo, Jeff Tumale, Sophia Sideri, Lucas Kapla, Sebastian Coman Photography & Jason Leung on Unsplash
Photo by Nathanaël Djimbilth

Midnight in Paris (*mood board spread*)
Photos by Justin Chrn, Latrach Med Jamil, Thomas de Luze, Guillaume Didelet (2 photos), NASA (2 photos) & Sander Dewerte on Unsplash
Map is from 1705
Photos by Nathanaël Djimbilth

Galaxy (*mood board spread*)
Photos by Fredrick Filix, NASA, Planet Volumes (2 photos), Jeremy Thomas (2 photos) & William Zhang on Unsplash
Photo by PA graphics for NASA
Headline by Jamie Carterfor Forbes

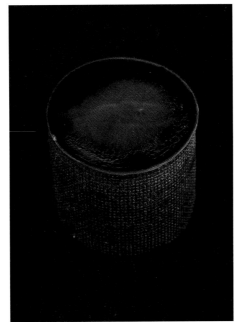

Colophon

Published by New Heroes & Pioneers

Text: Tal Spiegel
Photography: Nathanaël Djimbilth
Creative Direction: Francois Le Bled
Art Direction & Cover Design: Tal Spiegel
Graphic Design: Daniel Zachrisson
Copy Editing: Matt Porter, Roxanne Sancto & Francois Le Bled

Print and bound by BALTO print (Lithuania)
Legal deposit December 2022
ISBN: 978-91-986566-5-7

With special thanks to Cacao Barry

EXPRESS YOUR
TRUE NATURE™